TAKE TEN YEARS

1950s

KENT ARTS & LIBRARIES

REFERENCE COLLECTION

005467 6

Evans

EVANS BROTHERS LIMITED

Contents

The pictures on page 4 show
The Festival of Britain site, London
Police searching homes outside Nairobi, Kenya
Queen Elizabeth II's coronation
Stanley Matthews and the Stoke City football team
Churchill (second from left), with Eisenhower, Eden and Dulles, outside the White House, Washington, USA

The pictures on page 5 show
Khrushchev, Bulganin and Eden
Sputnik I
The first troops to arrive in Port Said
Harold Macmillan
Fidel Castro

Introduction

In 1950, the effects of World War II were still present. Major European cities had been badly bombed, and new houses, factories and shops had to be built. Food was still in short supply and rationing continued in Britain up until the mid-fifties.

There was much unrest in countries occupied by foreign rulers. In Africa, the British granted independence to the Gold Coast, and it became Ghana. Kenyans struggled for freedom and more land in a guerrilla war known as the Mau Mau rebellion. The Egyptians seized the Suez Canal, which the British and French had controlled for 75 years. The French had to leave Vietnam, and also faced guerrilla fighters in Algeria. The Tibetans resisted the Chinese, and the Hungarians tried to rid themselves of the Russians.

Many of these conflicts could have led to a third world war, as the superpowers took opposite sides. The dreadful threat of nuclear weapons may have averted war. Also, the United Nations was able to defuse some dangerous conflicts. But between East and West, the deadly Cold War continued. Towards the end of the decade this Cold War had thawed a little, but several smaller countries were still danger spots.

It was also a decade when mankind reached out for new knowledge. Nuclear power stations began to create electricity, but at the same time H-bombs were tested. People were nervous about the threat of nuclear war. Nobody wanted that. They were encouraged by the spectacular achievements in a new direction: the Russians launched the world's first artificial satellite, and the Americans trained astronauts for space flight. It seemed as if science fiction was coming true.

YEARS	WORLD AFFAIRS
1950	US and USSR are rivals; the US is afraid of Communist power in the East
1951	The Cold War: trials of suspected spies Baudouin becomes King of the Belgians
1952	Coup in Egypt Hussein becomes King of Jordan King George VI is succeeded by Queen Elizabeth II
1953	Queen crowned; she tours the Commonwealth Power struggle in USSR when Stalin dies
1954	Nasser leads Egyptian Republic SEATO formed Events in Vietnam may have a domino effect
1955	Warsaw Pact signed S. Vietnam becomes a Republic
1956	Nasser takes over Suez Canal Cold War begins to thaw
1957	Gold Coast becomes Ghana Common Market formed Russians launch Sputniks
1958	General de Gaulle is Premier of France Egypt and Syria become UAR King Feisal of Iraq murdered
1959	Castro takes over in Cuba The space race is on Dalai Lama flees from Tibet

WARS & REVOLTS	PEOPLE	EVENTS
The North Koreans invade South Korea	McCarthy accuses people of being Communists Frank Sinatra sings in London	The Stone of Scone is stolen Holy Year celebrated at the Vatican *Eagle* comic is launched
North Koreans pushed back	Maclean and Burgess disappear from British Foreign Office Churchill becomes Prime Minister again	The Festival of Britain
Mau Mau uprising in Kenya	Dr. Linse abducted in Berlin Agatha Christie's *Mousetrap* opens	Olympic Games in Finland Americans test H-bomb Coelacanth discovered
East German revolt	Hillary and Tenzing climb Everest Watson and Crick discover DNA Dr. Salk's polio vaccine	The Stanley Matthews Cup Final
French fight N. Vietnamese	Roger Bannister runs mile in 4 minutes Oppenheimer not allowed to see atomic secrets	Food rationing ends in Britain Rabbits killed by myxomatosis
Civil war in Cyprus	Martin Luther King leads fight against prejudice James Dean is killed	Bus boycott in Alabama First advertisements on TV in Britain
Hungarians revolt against Russian rule Conflict over Suez Spanish demonstrations against Franco	Khrushchev in England Grace Kelly becomes a Princess Archbishop Makarios exiled	Olympic Games in Australia *Under Milk Wood* performed Britain's first power station opened
	Beatniks in USA and England Macmillan becomes Prime Minister of Britain	Little Rock School admits black pupils
Civil war in Algeria	Pope John XXIII crowned Elvis Presley joins army Pasternak wins Nobel Prize	NASA opened in USA Jet service to USA begins Plane crash kills soccer players First Aldermaston march
Coup in Cuba More trouble in S. Vietnam	Khrushchev visits America Charles van Doren wins quizzes by fraud Makarios is President of Cyprus	Russians photograph other side of the moon Britain's first motorway

1950

THE WAR IN KOREA

NORTH KOREANS INVADE SOUTH

June 25, The Far East Korea is divided into two countries. North Korea is a Communist republic. South Korea is a democratic republic. The boundary between the two is the line of latitude 38°, known as the 38th parallel.

Today 60,000 North Korean soldiers, with Russian tanks and jet planes, crossed the 38th parallel, and invaded South Korea. The invasion has alarmed the Western powers. The United States helped South Korea after World War II. The USSR and the United States seem to be taking opposite sides in this dispute.

UNITED NATIONS STEPS IN

June 30, South Korea The North Korean army has captured South Korea's capital, Seoul. The South Koreans do not have a proper army, and their weapons are out of date. The United Nations has asked its members to help South Korea. The first American troops arrived today.

GENERAL MACARTHUR TAKES COMMAND

July 7, South Korea General MacArthur of the United States is commander of all forces in South Korea. Jet planes are bombing Pyongyang, the Northern capital. But the strong North Korean forces are resisting the UN army.

AMERICANS FORCED BACK TO PUSAN

Sept 1, South Korea The UN forces have been pushed right back to Pusan, on the south-east coast. Today they were joined by British troops. Their enemies, the North Koreans, began a terrific bombardment today along an 80-km (50-mile) front. The war is not going well for the UN forces.

UN troops in action in Korea

A SECOND FRONT IS OPENED

Sept 15, South Korea Over 250 ships have arrived at Inchon, on the west coast. They are troop carriers bringing in US soldiers. The country around Inchon is held by their enemies, the North Koreans. The US soldiers will fight their way towards Pusan. This will not be easy; the roads are mined and the opposition is very great. But it means that the enemy has to fight two armies.

UN FORCES ON THE OFFENSIVE

Oct 9, South Korea The troops from Inchon managed to reach Pusan. The two armies fought their way north and recaptured Seoul. Today they crossed the 38th parallel.

There is now a new threat, this time from China. President Chou En-lai said the UN troops had no right to invade North Korea.

UN FORCES HAVE TO WITHDRAW

Oct 27, North Korea At least 14 Chinese divisions have crossed into Korea. The UN forces are heavily outnumbered. Russian MiG planes are bombing their positions. They are retreating back towards the 38th parallel.

Korea is divided at the 38th parallel.

UN FORCES FACE DEFEAT

Dec 24, South Korea The UN army has lost all the ground it gained. In spite of this disaster, President Truman will not allow the army to use atomic bombs. The troops are back at the American base at Pusan.

CROWDS RECEIVE POPE'S BLESSING

July 9, Vatican City This is Holy Year for Roman Catholics. From all over the world pilgrims are coming to Rome. The Vatican staff have put up tents on the surrounding hills. One of the Fathers has been especially thoughtful to English visitors. He has arranged for a tea-room to be opened. He knows that to an English visitor a 'cuppa' is always welcome.

Today the Pope, Pius XII, blessed the huge crowd of pilgrims from an upper window of his residence in Vatican City.

His Holiness Pope Pius XII

SENATOR SEES REDS EVERYWHERE

Feb 20, Washington, USA A British nuclear scientist, Dr. Klaus Fuchs, has admitted that he supplied atomic secrets to the Russians. Suddenly Americans realize that the Russians may be making atomic bombs too. They are frightened of a nuclear war. Senator Joseph McCarthy is taking advantage of their fear. He accuses over 200 people in the State Department of being secret Communists. He gives no proof of this, but people believe him.

DISAPPEARANCE OF A STONE

Dec 29, Scotland The historic Stone of Scone is missing. This lump of sandstone sat under the Coronation chair in Westminster Abbey, London. It came from Scone in Scotland 650 years ago. An anonymous letter says the burglars will tell the police where it is, so long as the stone can stay in Scotland. The English are not likely to agree. Their kings and queens are crowned on the Stone of Scone. The police are searching for it in Scotland.

NEWS IN BRIEF . . .

HARRY LIME, MYSTERY MAN

Jan 13, London *The Third Man* opens in the West End today. It is a film about Harry Lime (played by Orson Welles), who is hunted through Vienna by his one-time friend. The hunt takes them through the sewers, and on a giant wheel at a fairground. The film has a haunting background tune, played on a zither.

SPACE IS AN EXCITING PLACE

April 14, London *Eagle*, a new strip cartoon weekly paper, is on sale for the first time today. On the front page Dan Dare and his fat friend Digby fight the forces of evil from other galaxies. Inside, Luck of the Legion fights with desert 'baddies', cowboys battle with Indians, and highwaymen lurk in the shadows. The drawings by Frank Hampson are superb. *Eagle* is on sale every Friday, price threepence.

The front page of the *Eagle*

NEAT AND SMART IS FASHIONABLE

Spring, London Nylon stockings are as popular as ever. They are held up with suspenders from the new elastic roll-on girdles. These are a perfect foundation for Dior's sheath dresses and tailored skirts. For dancing, wide skirts over several petticoats are set off by a wide belt. Blouses are soft nylon. Make-up is very important for eyes and lips. Nail varnish matches the lipstick.

Young men on the dance floor wear suits and ties. The Fifty-Shilling Tailor, with branches in every town, can supply a ready-to-wear suit for under £3. A girl likes her escort to look smart.

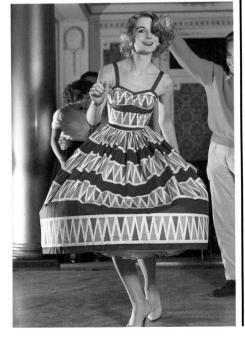

SINGER DELIGHTS HIS FANS

July 15, London Frank Sinatra is singing to packed audiences in London this week. He is the most popular singer in the United States. Bing Crosby once said, "He has the voice of a lifetime – but why did it have to happen in mine?"

1951

SPIES AND SUSPECTED SPIES

HISS'S APPEAL FAILS

March 12, New York Last year Alger Hiss, an American lawyer, denied in court that he spied for Russia. The court found Hiss not guilty, but said he had lied while under oath. He was sentenced to five years in prison. Hiss appealed, but today the appeal court has not reduced his sentence. People still wonder if he was in fact a spy.

FOREIGN OFFICE MEN DISAPPEAR

June 8, London Two senior Foreign Office officials, Donald Maclean and Guy Burgess, have been missing since Friday May 25. On the following Monday, officers from the British secret service were going to question Maclean. They suspected him of spying for the USSR. The government is wondering whether someone warned Maclean. Police are searching for them all over Europe.

POLICE QUESTION A THIRD MAN

Nov 30, London An inquiry has opened into the Burgess and Maclean affair. A diplomat named Kim Philby was recalled from his job at the British Embassy in Washington to answer questions. Guy Burgess stayed in Philby's house there. As a senior Foreign Office official, Philby knew Maclean was going to be questioned in May. The inquiry found nothing to suggest that he was guilty.

ROSENBERGS FOUND GUILTY

April 5, New York Julius and Ethel Rosenberg have been sentenced to death for spying for Russia. They are accused of obtaining information about the atomic bomb in 1944. David Greenglass, who worked on the bomb project, passed information to Rosenberg. He passed it on to an agent named Harry Gold. Greenglass and Gold confessed, but the Rosenbergs said they were innocent. The Rosenbergs are Communists. Their lawyer says they cannot get a fair trial because of Senator McCarthy's anti-Communist activities.

Ethel and Julius Rosenberg after their trial

THE GIs ARE COMING BACK

June 18, London The British government will allow the United States to build an air base in England. It will be at Greenham Common in Berkshire. The Americans will have fighter and bomber planes here permanently. The local householders are not happy with this decision.

FESTIVAL A TONIC TO THE NATION

June 1, London The Festival of Britain is raising our spirits with its colour and gaiety. All along the South Bank of the River Thames, mudflats have been drained and old houses pulled down. In their place is an elegant collection of buildings. A magnificent new concert hall seats 3000 people. The biggest dome ever built covers the Dome of Discovery. It is like a mushroom on thin legs. There is a crazy railway and a children's zoo. The tall thin needle is called the Skylon. It is lit up at night, and is a symbol of the future. The Festival Gardens and funfair are extremely popular. This is the first large leisure park in Britain.

The Festival of Britain site with the Skylon

BELGIANS WELCOME KING BAUDOUIN

July 16, Brussels King Leopold III of the Belgians has abdicated (resigned). The Belgians think he should not have surrendered to the Germans in 1940. There have been riots and strikes against him. His very popular first wife, Queen Astrid, died in a car crash in 1935. Her elder son will become King Baudouin I.

NORTH KOREANS PUSHED BACK

July 10, Korea Talks are going on to try to end the Korean war. All through the first months of this year battles raged in South Korea. By April the UN army had forced the North Koreans and Chinese back over the 38th parallel.

President Truman dismissed General MacArthur because he wanted to march his men into China. Such action might start a third world war. Casualties in Korea are heavy, and include hundreds of civilians.

SPANIARDS WANT THEIR ROCK BACK

Aug 5, Barcelona Today has been proclaimed Gibraltar Day. Gibraltar has been a British possession since the 17th century. This angers the Spanish, who say that it is part of Spain. They will mark this day every year until they get the Rock back.

CHURCHILL BACK IN PARLIAMENT

Oct 26, London The British people have voted for a Conservative government. Mr. Winston Churchill is Prime Minister once more. Under the Labour government of 1945–51, many industries were nationalized. The Conservatives may return some of them to private companies.

Mrs. Churchill laughs as her husband Winston gives his famous victory salute.

PERÓN BACK IN POWER

Nov 11, Buenos Aires, Argentina Colonel Juan Perón has been re-elected President of Argentina. He first came to power in 1945. Perón is very popular with working people. His wife Eva (Evita) has worked tirelessly among them. Her influence has won him many votes at election time. But the economy of the country is weak, and Perón has an added burden: his wife is very ill with cancer.

Juan and Eva Perón wave to the crowd at Buenos Aires.

NEWS IN BRIEF . . .

FAMILY LIFE TODAY

Sept 30, New York and London Many towns are spreading outwards as houses are built in the suburbs. In America, new houses are being fitted with central heating for the first time. The heating is fuelled by oil or by gas. Suburban homes are bought by young couples with children. Usually the husband goes out to work while his wife looks after the children and does the housework. Many more people are marrying young these days.

GOOD FAMILY ENTERTAINMENT

Dec 15, New York Singing cowboy Gene Autry has swept to fame with a song that is out just in time for Christmas. It is called 'Rudolf the Red-Nosed Reindeer'. Home entertainment is booming. The number of TV sets has increased. As a result 3000 cinemas have had to close. The movie industry has to produce better films to keep its audience. This year Marilyn Monroe has made *The Asphalt Jungle* and Bette Davis stars in *All About Eve*. In America you can visit a drive-in cinema. From your car, you can watch the movie on a huge screen.

On a night out at a drive-in movie

1952

MAU MAU IN KENYA
AFRICANS WANT MORE LAND

Jan 1, Nairobi At the beginning of this century, British settlers were given farms in Kenya. They enclosed their lands and would not allow strangers onto them. This is against African custom. Africans say that land belongs to everyone. Their population has increased, partly because of European medicine. Available land has become scarce.

A group of black nationalists has formed the Kenya African Union (KAU). They want the white government to give Africans more land. The nationalists sing a song which, translated, means: 'Mother, whether you cry or not, I will only come back when our lands are returned; when I obtain our lands and African freedom.'

OATH-TAKING IN KIKUYULAND

Aug 24, Nairobi A secret society called Mau Mau is recruiting Africans of the Kikuyu tribe. Recruits are forced to swear an oath that they will murder people if asked to. The Kikuyu believe that oaths are very powerful, and they will die if they break one. Most recruits are too frightened to protest. Oath-givers are touring the Kikuyu districts near Nairobi, recruiting for Mau Mau.

Jomo Kenyatta (in light trousers) pictured at the funeral ceremony of Chief Waruhiu. Mr. Kenyatta is President of the KAU and is also suspected of being a Mau Mau leader.

FUNERAL OF KIKUYU CHIEF

Oct 14, Nairobi Sir Evelyn Baring (the Governor of Kenya), Jomo Kenyatta (the President of the KAU), and members of the government were among the hundreds of mourners at the funeral of Kikuyu Chief Waruhiu. A week ago three gunmen shot him dead. Police believe the gunmen were Mau Mau, who have already murdered over 40 Kikuyu. A few days before his death Chief Waruhiu condemned Mau Mau violence.

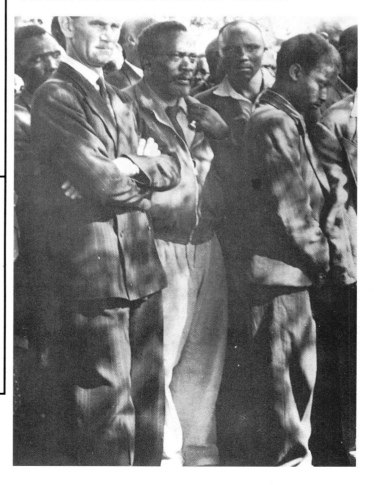

STATE OF EMERGENCY IN KENYA

Oct 21, Nairobi Sir Evelyn Baring has declared a State of Emergency. British troops are coming to Kenya. They will search for the Mau Mau, who are living rough in the forests and hills. Others who have taken the oath stay in the towns. They supply the terrorists with food and information. Town-dwellers suspected of being Mau Mau have been rounded up.

Jomo Kenyatta has been arrested. The government thinks that the KAU is organizing Mau Mau.

British troops guard Kenyan villagers during a search for hidden Mau Mau weapons.

SAD NEWS REACHES KENYA

Feb 6, Nairobi Princess Elizabeth learnt tonight of the death of her father, King George VI. She has become Queen Elizabeth II of England. The Princess and Prince Philip arrived last night at the famous 'Treetops' lodge in Kenya. Armed game wardens protected the couple from a herd of elephants as they walked through the forest to the tree-house. During the night they saw in a floodlit clearing two waterbuck fighting each other to the death. Treetops' visitors book records that on this day a young woman climbed into the tree as a princess, and climbed down from the tree a queen.

PROMINENT WEST GERMAN ABDUCTED

July 8, West Berlin Berlin is surrounded by East Germany. The city is divided between the Russians, the Americans, the French and the British. Dr. Walter Linse, a lawyer living in Berlin, has told people about the cruelty taking place in East Germany. Today Dr. Linse was kidnapped in broad daylight. He was shot in the leg and bundled into a car. East German guards at the border closed the barrier after the kidnap car had passed.

The East Germans have put up double barbed wire fences along the frontier with West Germany.

Princess Elizabeth and the Duke of Edinburgh at the Sagana River in the Kenyan highlands

KING FAROUK TOLD TO LEAVE

July 23, Cairo There has been a coup in Egypt. A group of young army officers has deposed King Farouk. Their leader is called Jamal Abd al-Nasser. King Farouk lived in luxury, and did not tackle his country's problems.

The rebels have set up a Revolutionary Council. General Neguib, head of the armed forces, will lead it. The Council will expel Europeans from top government jobs. They want the British army to leave the Suez Canal Zone. The British are alarmed at these decisions.

HEROES OF THE OLYMPICS

Aug 3, Helsinki On July 19 a 55-year-old runner lit the Olympic torch to open the Olympic Games. The Finns gave him a great welcome. In 1920 and 1924 he was their Olympic hero. His name is Paavo Nurmi.

The Russians took part in the games for the first time since 1912. Two of their female competitors won gold medals. But this year's hero was Emil Zatopek of Czechoslovakia. He created Olympic records for the marathon, and the 10,000 and 5000 metre events. His wife Dana won the medal for women's javelin throwing.

A young woman dressed in white tried to take advantage of this meeting of East and West. At the opening ceremony she ran forward to plead for world peace. She was turned away from the microphone, her message unspoken.

SCHOOLBOY BECOMES KING

Aug 11, London Crown Prince Hussein is 15 years old, and at school in England. Today he has become the King of Jordan. His grandfather, King Abdallah, was shot dead in Jerusalem a year ago. He created the state of Jordan from the old Transjordan and central Palestine. The new King wants to finish his education in Britain. Until he returns home, Jordan will be ruled by a council of three people.

NEW BOMB WILL BE DEADLY

Nov 30, Washington United States scientists wore special dark glasses to watch tests on a new atomic bomb. The bomb is hundreds of times more powerful than those dropped on Japan in 1945. It is called an H-bomb (H is for hydrogen). Radioactive dust rose in a huge cloud 40 km (24 miles) high and 160 km (100 miles) wide. The tests were carried out on an uninhabited island in the Pacific. After the explosion, the island had completely disappeared. The Russians may also be working on an H-bomb. In the West, some people are building bomb shelters in their gardens.

The newly-crowned King on a visit to Rome

NEWS IN BRIEF . . .

OPERA GAINS A NEW WORK

Feb 28, London Benjamin Britten conducted his new opera, *Billy Budd*, this month at Covent Garden Opera House. The opera takes place on board an 18th-century naval ship. It tells the sad story of a sailor who accidentally kills an officer who is tormenting him. The tenor Peter Pears sings the leading role.

THE MOUSETRAP OPENS

Nov 25, London *The Mousetrap* opened last night in the West End. Agatha Christie, the author, has already written many detective novels. In this play, she keeps the audience guessing to the last. The detective, who works out which of many snowbound characters had the motive, the means and the opportunity, is played by Richard Attenborough. Sheila Sim plays a leading role. If you want to know 'whodunnit', you will have to go along to the Ambassador's Theatre and find out.

AMERICAN IS WORLD CHAMPION

Sept 24, Philadelphia Rocky Marciano is the new world heavyweight boxing champion. Last night he knocked out 'Jersey' Joe Walcott after 13 rounds. In the first round Rocky was behind on points. But he recovered, and used his hard-hitting technique to batter the former champion. Rocky learnt to box in the army during the war. Before he took up boxing seriously, his first love was baseball.

3-D MOVIES HERE TO STAY?

Nov 26, Los Angeles Film-goers have to wear special glasses to see the latest movie, *B'wana Devil*. One lens is red, the other green. The glasses make the film seem to be three-dimensional. This could cause panic – in *B'wana Devil* lions appear to leap out of the screen! We shall see whether 3-D movies catch on, or if this is just a new gimmick.

LONDON'S AIR CAN KILL

Nov 31, London November is always a bad month for fog. But we now have 'smog'. The mixture of fog and smoke from factories and home coal fires is causing alarm. It is killing old people, young children, and those with asthma. The government is looking for ways of stopping this deadly form of air pollution.

UNUSUAL FISH IS RARE SURVIVAL FROM STONE AGE

Dec 29, Madagascar A fisherman has caught a very strange fish in the Indian Ocean. It is called a coelacanth. Fossil remains of the fish have been found in rocks. Scientists thought the fish became extinct about 50 million years ago!

1953

FIRST YEAR OF A NEW REIGN
PREPARATIONS FOR GREAT DAY

May 30, London Everyone is preparing for the Queen's coronation. The streets of London are decorated. Ten thousand servicemen have practised marching in procession. Two thousand bandsmen are perfecting their music, and 250 police horses are groomed daily. Overseas politicians and colonial rulers are arriving in London. Queen Elizabeth has asked for the route to be longer than usual so that more children can see the procession. Queen Elizabeth and Prince Philip have two children, Prince Charles and Princess Anne.

THE QUEEN IS CROWNED

June 2, London The New Elizabethan Age began today when Queen Elizabeth II was crowned in Westminster Abbey. Her golden coach was drawn by eight white horses. At the climax of the long ceremony, the Archbishop of Canterbury put the crown on her head. One royal visitor pleased the London crowd above all others. This was Queen Salote of Tonga, an island in the Pacific. Her warm personality and beaming smile drew cheers from the onlookers.

All over the country people are attending street parties and band concerts. In the evening most towns have dances and firework displays. It has been a cold rainy day, but this has not dampened the general excitement.

CLIMBERS ON ROOF OF THE WORLD

May 29, Nepal   At 11.30 this morning two climbers made history. Edmund Hillary of New Zealand, and Tenzing Norgay of Nepal have reached the summit of Mount Everest. Sir John Hunt led the party of 10 British and 36 Nepalese climbers. Yesterday Hillary and Tenzing camped at a point nearly 9000 metres (27,900 ft) up the mountain. The temperature was −27°C, and the wind rose at times to gale force. At the top of Everest, Tenzing buried gifts of food to the god of the mountain, and Hillary buried a small crucifix.

Edmund Hillary (left) and Tenzing Norgay on Everest

THE VIEW FROM EVEREST

'I was beginning to tire a little now. I had been cutting steps continuously for two hours and Tenzing, too, was moving very slowly . . . I wondered rather dully just how long we could keep it up. . . I then realized that the ridge ahead, instead of still monotonously rising, now dropped sharply away. . A few more whacks of the ice-axe in the firm snow and we stood on top.

My initial feelings were of relief – relief that there were no more steps to cut – no more ridges to traverse and no more humps to tantalize us with hopes of success. I looked at Tenzing and in spite of the balaclava, goggles and oxygen mask all encrusted with long icicles that concealed his face, there was no disguising his infectious grin of pure delight as he looked all around him. We shook hands and then Tenzing threw his arm around my shoulders and we thumped each other on the back until we were almost breathless. It was 11.30 a.m.'

(Edmund Hillary, from *The Ascent of Everest* by John Hunt, Hodder & Stoughton 1953)

ROYAL COUPLE TOUR COMMONWEALTH

Dec 25, Auckland, New Zealand   The Queen broadcast her Christmas message to the Commonwealth today from New Zealand. She and Prince Philip have been away from England for over a month. They started their tour in the West Indies. On the Pacific island of Tonga they met Queen Salote again. The royal couple will visit Australia, Aden and Uganda. In May they will board *Britannia* in the Mediterranean for the journey home.

The royal couple with Queen Salote of Tonga, an island in the Pacific Ocean

NEW PRESIDENT RESISTS SOVIETS

Jan 13, Belgrade, Yugoslavia Josip Tito has become President of Yugoslavia. He is the country's first Communist president. Stalin wanted Yugoslavia to be under Soviet control. Tito has resisted him. Yugoslavia will remain a neutral country – though its policies are like those of the USSR.

AFRICAN LEADER IS EXILED

Nov 30, Kampala, Uganda The Kabaka (King) of Buganda, Mutesa II, has been forced to leave Uganda by the British. Buganda is the country of the Ganda people. It forms a quarter of the British territory of Uganda. When self-government comes, the Ganda want Buganda to be a separate country. They are furious that their King has been exiled.

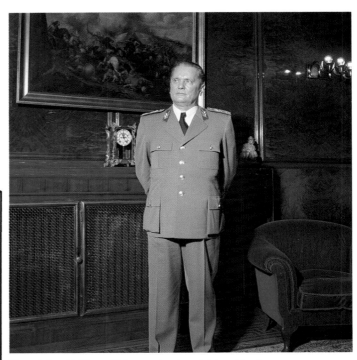

President Tito of Yugoslavia at his villa home

TANKS HALT EAST GERMAN REVOLT

June 21, Berlin The East Germans live under Soviet rule. They have gone on strike against longer hours of work, and the low standard of living. Thousands of German prisoners of war are still in Russia. The rioters demanded their return. They tore down Communist flags in the city.

It is the first time a country has revolted against Soviet occupation. Usually people are too frightened to do so. The Russians have sent tanks into the streets of East Germany to restore order.

SCIENTISTS FIND 'SECRET OF LIFE'

April 25, Cambridge We have known for some years that our height, looks, brain power, and everything about us depends on our genes. We inherit our genes from our parents. J.D.Watson and F.H.C. Crick of the University of Cambridge have discovered that genes are made of a chemical called DNA. DNA has a structure like a twisted ladder, which splits in half when a cell divides.

Demonstrators in East Berlin attack Soviet tanks.

VILLAGERS MASSACRED IN KENYA

Sept 15, Lari village, Kenya After a long trial, Jomo Kenyatta has been sentenced to seven years hard labour. He denied he was leading the Mau Mau, and his arrest has not stopped their attacks. They have destroyed 150 schools and killed 32 teachers. Last night they murdered nearly 100 men, women and children by setting fire to a whole village.

Many Kikuyu are against the Mau Mau. They have joined the Kikuyu Guard to protect their families. They show great bravery, because Guard posts are obvious targets for Mau Mau attacks.

USSR HAS NO FIRM LEADER

Dec 23, Moscow Stalin's death on March 5 was followed by a power struggle in the USSR. At that time Lavrenti Beria, the chief of the secret police, had immense power. But so had other leaders, including Molotov, Malenkov and Khrushchev. Beria is the first one to 'disappear'. Malenkov accused him of being a Western spy and trying to seize power. Today he was executed. The Russians hardly care who finally becomes sole leader. Forced labour, concentration camps and the dreaded secret police still dominate their lives.

NEWS IN BRIEF . . .

SEARCHING THE SEA BED

Jan 15, Switzerland A 70-year-old Swiss scientist, Auguste Piccard, has dived in a bathyscaphe of his own design to the bottom of the Mediterranean. He reached a depth of 3.5 km (2 miles). The fish down there live in darkness. Professor Piccard has explored not only the depths but also the heights: 22 years ago he reached the stratosphere in a balloon.

THE STANLEY MATTHEWS FINAL

May 29, London From high on Everest, Hillary and Tenzing today tuned their radio to the BBC. They heard tremendous excitement coming from Wembley Stadium. Two minutes before the end of the match, the score in the FA Cup Final stood at 3–2 to Bolton Wanderers. Then suddenly Blackpool's Stanley Matthews put on a terrific spurt. And in that last two minutes his footwork allowed Blackpool to score two goals and win the cup. The crowd cheered itself hoarse.

CRIPPLING DISEASE ATTACKED

March 26, New York The most feared disease today is poliomielitis (polio). Many victims die. Some have to use an 'iron lung', which helps their paralysed lungs to breathe. Others are crippled for life. Now at last a scientist, Dr. J. Salk, has vaccinated a group of children, to prevent them getting the disease.

TV NEWS IN BLACK AND WHITE

June 3, London About 25 million people watched the Coronation on TV; from their homes, their pubs and clubs, or their community halls. People who waited in the streets from dawn to see the Queen pass said that they preferred live action: TV shows things in black and white – they saw the procession in colour!

Stanley Matthews after his team's victory in the FA Cup Final

1954

VIETNAM AND THE FRENCH

FRENCH HOLDING VIETNAM

Jan 1, Dien Bien Phu, Vietnam   Since 1945 the French have occupied a part of north Vietnam. Vietnamese Communists, the Viet Minh, want the French to leave. Their forces are led by General Giap. The country around Dien Bien Phu is mountainous, and thickly forested.

Last November the French dropped paratroops in the north-west of Vietnam, and captured Dien Bien Phu. They thought that guerrillas would come down in small groups from the mountains, and be easy targets to attack. But General Giap was cleverer than that. He has led a huge army to the outskirts of Dien Bien Phu. His soldiers even dragged field guns over the mountains. And 20,000 men with equipment on bicycles followed through the narrow jungle paths. It is clear that General Giap means to oust the French garrison from their stronghold position.

VIET MINH ENTER TOWN

May 8, Dien Bien Phu   After a siege lasting 55 days, the French have finally been defeated by the Viet Minh. The French garrison of about 19,000 men was completely surrounded. The French did not hold any of the territory round Dien Bien Phu, so there was nowhere for them to go. Those who survived the siege surrendered to General Giap's North Vietnamese troops. It seems that after this heavy defeat, France has no future in Indo-China.

1954 VIETNAM

During the course of this year, Vietnam was divided into two countries.

VIETNAM TO BE DIVIDED

July 21, Geneva   The United Nations has ruled that Vietnam should be divided into two countries. The northern part, where all the fighting has taken place, is to be called North Vietnam. Its capital will be Hanoi. Ho Chi Minh, the Communist leader of the Viet Minh, will be its President. His rule will end at latitude 17°, the '17th parallel'. South of this is South Vietnam. It will be ruled by Emperor Bao Dai. The French will support his government.

Ho Chi Minh, leader of the Viet Minh

FAMILIES MOVE TO THE SOUTH

Oct 8, Vietnam   Thousands of refugees are leaving North Vietnam and going to the South. President Eisenhower of the United States has sent American ships to transport them by sea. He says that Communist gains in south-east Asia have 'a domino effect': when one country falls, the second, third and fourth need less and less pressure to fall too. He does not like to see a Communist government in North Vietnam.

THE WITCH-HUNT IS OVER

Dec 2, Washington   Mr. McCarthy's fellow Senators have finally turned against him. He has called too many innocent people Communist, or un-American. In the past four years he has charged two presidents with treason, threatened the army chiefs, and recruited hundreds of anti-Communist spies. Because of him 600 college professors have been dismissed.

SEATO AIDS PEACEFUL DEVELOPMENT

Sept 8, Manila, Philippines   Eight countries have agreed to join together to keep the peace in south-east Asia. They will also send south-east Asian countries money for their development. The members of SEATO (South-East Asia Treaty Organization) are the United States, Britain, France, Pakistan, Australia, New Zealand, Thailand and the Philippines. They will meet next year.

TROOPS TO LEAVE SUEZ

July 27, Cairo   The British have agreed that troops will leave the Suez Canal Zone over the next two years. They will only return if a Middle Eastern country tries to invade Egypt. The agreement was signed with Colonel Nasser, who has taken over from General Neguib. Last May he declared the country a republic. His policy to end imperialism is known to all Egyptians; his new radio station broadcasts his socialist and anti-Western views.

British troops beside the Suez Canal

MAU MAU REVENGE ATTACK

May 26, Nairobi, Kenya 'Treetops', which the Queen visited last year, has been burnt to the ground. One of Treetops' lorry-drivers was a member of Mau Mau. For several months he drove food and other supplies into the forest. Armed Africans were waiting. They took the supplies to the Mau Mau in the mountains. When the British discovered this, they tried to ambush the armed men. The ambush failed. The Mau Mau took their revenge by burning the tourist lodge. Royal Air Force planes are trying to bomb the Mau Mau out of the Aberdares mountain range.

THE POWER OF A NUCLEAR BLAST

June 29, Washington Last month the United States exploded another H-bomb. The test took place on the island of Bikini. The bomb's power was so great that fishermen in a boat 112 km (68 miles) away were badly affected by radiation sickness.

People all over the world are extremely frightened in case war breaks out between two countries with H-bombs. The leading American scientist, Dr. Robert Oppenheimer, would like to ban them. He helped to develop nuclear bombs. Now he is no longer allowed to work on atomic projects because of his views.

NEWS IN BRIEF . . .

ATHLETE IN FOUR-MINUTE MILE

May 6, Oxford For years runners have been trying to run a mile in less than four minutes. Today 25-year-old Roger Bannister has set a new record of 3 minutes 59.4 seconds. He is very interested in the whole subject of running – how to get the best out of yourself. He trains carefully.

The record-breaking moment as Roger Bannister crosses the winning line.

RABBITS MUST GO, SAY FARMERS

June 30, Britain Farmers hate rabbits. They damage young trees, and nibble grass down to ground level. When this happens, moss takes over, and sheep won't eat moss.

But now the rabbits have a deadly enemy. It is a virus called myxomatosis. It is killing thousands of rabbits. Although they have to be controlled, it is distressing to see them suffering from this disease.

YOU CAN BUY FOOD FREELY NOW

July 3, London Food rationing has finally ended. You may burn your ration books! Shops are now more plentifully stocked, and luxury items are returning to the shelves. We seem to be eating less red meat and more chicken. We eat less sugar than before the war – even though sweets have not been rationed for a year. There are some new imported fruits in the shops, and more people are drinking coffee.

WHERE WINE FLOWS LIKE WATER

Oct 15, France The grape harvest is attracting a lot of casual labour. The grapes are made into wine, which is one of France's most famous exports. It is also a Frenchman's daily drink. Doctors say a man should drink no more than one litre of red wine a day. Many drink a lot more than that, especially in rural areas. The government is starting a campaign to warn people of the danger of heavy drinking.

1955

CIVIL WAR IN CYPRUS
ISLANDERS WANT UNION WITH GREECE

Jan 1, Nicosia, Cyprus The island of Cyprus is ruled by the British. Although it lies just south of Turkey, more Greeks live here than Turks. Cypriot Greeks want Cyprus to be part of Greece. They call this union *enosis*. Five years ago they gained a powerful leader. He is Archbishop Makarios, head of the Greek Church in Cyprus. Athens radio encourages Cypriot Greeks to fight for *enosis*.

FIGHTING BREAKS OUT IN CYPRUS

June 30, Nicosia A Greek army officer, Colonel George Grivas, has recruited hundreds of young Greeks into a guerrilla army. They are called EOKA, which in Greek stands for National Organization of Cypriot Struggle. They are burning buildings in Nicosia, the capital of the country, and in the eastern town of Famagusta. A large number of Turkish civilians have been murdered, and their homes and farms destroyed.

BRITISH IN CONFLICT WITH EOKA

Nov 28, Nicosia The British government has declared a state of emergency in Cyprus. This means that the Governor may deport or arrest anyone who disturbs the peace. Only the British may be armed. This comes after months of heavy fighting. British commando troops were flown in. They have been searching for guerrillas in the mountains. Hundreds have already been arrested. If they are convicted of planting bombs or of murder they are executed.

There is still intense fighting in the streets of Famagusta. The troops are calling this the 'Murder mile'. The British blame Archbishop Makarios for supporting Colonel Grivas and the EOKA. This is one more British territory that is causing trouble. But if the British leave, the Greeks and Turks will still be at loggerheads. The British government hopes to solve the crisis before withdrawing.

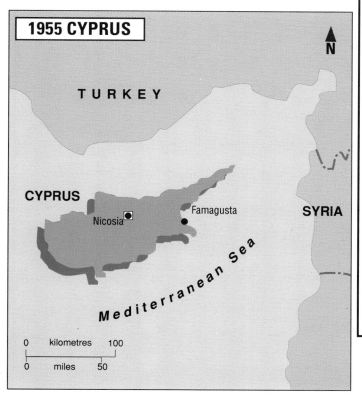

1955 CYPRUS

N

TURKEY

CYPRUS

Nicosia

Famagusta

SYRIA

Mediterranean Sea

| 0 | kilometres | 100 |
| 0 | miles | 50 |

Although close to Turkey, Cyprus is a largely Greek island, under British rule.

THE WARSAW PACT SIGNED

May 14, Warsaw   The Soviet Union and seven other Eastern European countries have made a pact to help one another. If one country is attacked, the rest will go to its defence. But they are agreed that disarmament is necessary for world peace. The Russians organized the Pact as an association similar to NATO, the alliance to which Western countries belong. The headquarters of the Warsaw Pact is in Moscow.

The Warsaw Pact committee with Soviet ministers Marshall Zhukov, Mr. Molotov and Marshall Konyev of the joint armed forces

BLACK AMERICANS BOYCOTT BUSES

Dec 5, Montgomery, Alabama   Black Americans have sworn to walk or cycle to work instead of going by bus. Last Thursday a young black dressmaker got on a bus after doing her Christmas shopping. The back of the bus, where blacks are supposed to sit, was full. She sat in a 'whites' only' seat. As the bus filled, the driver called "Niggers move back". The young lady stayed where she was. She was arrested and fined.

Over the weekend a young black clergyman, Dr. Martin Luther King, organized a bus boycott. Nobody knows much about him, but his message is love and understanding: "Don't ever let anyone pull you so low as to make you hate them," he says. The boycott is attracting attention all over the United States, as a form of peaceful protest.

PRINCESS MARGARET NOT TO MARRY

Oct 31, London   Princess Margaret's romance with Group Captain Peter Townsend is over. She has decided not the marry the former airforce officer. Members of the royal family do not usually marry without the Queen's consent. Peter Townsend is divorced, and this would make it difficult for the Queen to give her consent. She is Head of the Anglican Church, whose marriage service contains the words 'till death us do part'. If Princess Margaret had married Townsend she would have given up her place as third in line to the throne.

Princess Margaret with Group Captain Townsend in South Africa

SOUTH VIETNAM IS A REPUBLIC

Oct 26, Saigon   The Emperor of South Vietnam, Bao Dai, lives in the south of France. He left the government of the country to his ministers. In April rebels started a civil war in Saigon, the capital. They defeated the government, and today they declared South Vietnam a republic. Its first president is Ngo Dinh Diem.

BURGESS AND MACLEAN NEWS

Sept 18, London A Russian has published an article in a British newspaper. It is about the missing Foreign Office men, Guy Burgess and Donald Maclean. They are in the Soviet Union. The article claims they were recruited as Russian spies while they were at Cambridge University in the 1930s. Nobody has discovered yet who is the 'third man' who warned them to leave England.

Guy Burgess   Donald Maclean

NEWS IN BRIEF . . .

LITTLE MO IS TO RETIRE

Feb 22, New York Maureen Connolly is going to retire from tennis championships. She was only 16 when in 1951 she won the US women's tennis tournament. Little Mo, as she was called, also drew crowds to Wimbledon's centre court. She won the women's singles three years in succession. During those years she also won three US championships. Little Mo is a great horse rider. But last year she had a fall and injured her leg. She has not played in tennis tournaments since then. Now she plans to coach other players.

ACTOR KILLED IN ROAD ACCIDENT

Sept 30, Los Angeles James Dean was the hero of countless teenage movie fans. He has died today in a car crash at the age of 24. His latest film has not yet been released. Called *Rebel Without a Cause*, it is about a rich young man who is angry and frustrated with life. James Dean's death brings to an end a promising career, which began with a part in the film *East of Eden*.

THIS YEAR'S FASHION TIP

July 31, London Young men are rebelling against traditional gear. They choose clothes that copy those of King Edward VII's day – which is why they are called 'Teddy boys'. There is a brisk trade in long jackets with velvet collars, brocade waistcoats, bootlace ties, narrow trousers and 'winkle-picker' shoes. 'Teds' let their hair grow long and leave their sideburns intact.

Mary Quant's new shop called Bazaar in Chelsea sells straight shifts in synthetic materials for the girls. They wear them with plastic costume jewellery. And a new fashion has arrived from America – skin-tight jeans. Jeans were first worn by miners in the United States, but here it is the girls who are buying and wearing them.

Teddy boys in London

IT PAYS TO ADVERTISE

Sept 22, London At 8.15 p.m. you will be able to see the first ever advertisement to appear on British television. It encourages you to buy Gibbs SR toothpaste, and shows a toothbrush and toothpaste tube in a block of ice. Viewers are looking forward to watching the new independent channel (ITV).

CROCKETT BOOM ENDS

Dec 15, London The craze for Davy Crockett hats is over. Christmas shoppers are looking for other attractions. The trade in coon-skins boomed for six months as children dressed like their hero. The real Davy Crockett was an American hunter who died in 1836. His picture shows him dressed in a fur hat with a tail. Now the King of the Wild Frontier is becoming just a legend once more.

1956

THE SUEZ CRISIS

NASSER TAKES OVER CANAL

July 26, Suez, Egypt   Colonel Nasser has nationalized the Suez Canal. He announced this after Britain and America decided not to pay for Egypt's new Aswan Dam. With the money the canal earns, the Egyptians will be able to pay for the dam themselves. The British and French say that Nasser's action is unlawful.

PILOTS WALK OUT

Sept 14, Suez   Today British and French pilots walked out of their jobs on the Suez Canal. The Egyptians have only a few trained pilots of their own. It is a highly specialized job. The Egyptian pilots say that they will work long hours without extra pay. They will train new recruits. Colonel Nasser says he will never use foreign pilots again.

ISRAELIS THREATEN EGYPT

Oct 30, Suez   Yesterday Israeli troops marched towards the canal from the east. They said they were trying to stop the Egyptians raiding Israeli territory. The British and French demanded that both Israelis and Egyptians withdraw, leaving a no-man's-land of 16 km (10 miles) on each side of the canal. The Israelis have agreed, but the Egyptians have not. Some people think the British government encouraged the Israelis to invade.

EGYPTIANS BLOCK THE CANAL

Nov 6, Suez   The Egyptians have sunk several ships in the canal, and completely blocked it. All ships will now have to travel right round Africa. This adds 10,000 km (6000 miles) to their journey.

British aircraft have bombed military targets in Egypt. The British and French dropped paratroops in the area. The Israelis are again advancing towards the canal. The United Nations has asked all foreign troops to leave Egypt at once.

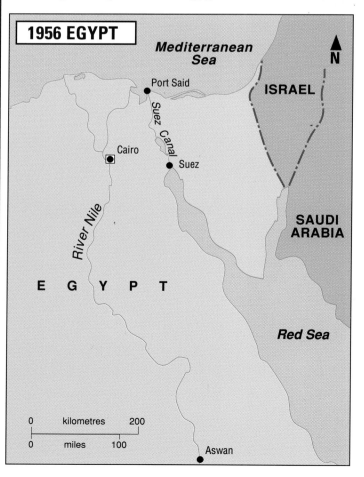

1956 EGYPT

Mediterranean Sea
Port Said
ISRAEL
Suez Canal
Cairo
Suez
River Nile
EGYPT
SAUDI ARABIA
Red Sea
0 kilometres 200
0 miles 100
Aswan

HUNGARY FIGHTS FOR FREEDOM

Oct 31, Budapest, Hungary   Last week a huge crowd of people gathered in Budapest's main square. They demanded that Russian troops leave Hungary. Since the war Russian secret police have been spying on Hungarians. Nobody had any freedom of speech or action. Now people have brought out national flags that have been hidden for years. They have destroyed a huge bronze statue of Stalin in the city centre.

Rioters entered the prison and freed Cardinal Mindszenty, the head of the Roman Catholic Church in Hungary. He was sentenced by the Russians to life imprisonment in 1949.

Demonstrators in Hungary pulled down a huge statue of Stalin.

RUSSIANS RETURN IN FORCE

Nov 5, Budapest   After just five days of freedom, Hungary is once again under the Russian heel. Yesterday Soviet planes bombed the centre of Budapest. A thousand tanks flattened houses and fired on civilians. Mr. Khrushchev says that the troops were invited back by loyal Hungarian Communists.

The Hungarians fought bitterly and bravely, but they did not have the power to resist. Cardinal Mindszenty is safe in the American Embassy. Professional guides are charging high prices to lead over 200,000 refugees across the border into Yugoslavia and Austria. The route to freedom is dangerous because it is heavily mined.

UN FORCES ARRIVE AT SUEZ

Nov 21, Suez   A United Nations peace-keeping force has arrived at Suez to take over control of the region. It will take several months before the canal can be used again. The Americans blame the British for handling the affair badly.

The first UN troops arrive in Port Said, Egypt.

EX-CHIEF RETURNS TO AFRICA

April 8, Gaberones, Bechuanaland   Seretse Khama has returned to the country of his birth, Bechuanaland [Botswana]. In 1948 he married an English girl, Ruth Williams. The marriage dismayed his people, the Bamangwato. Seretse Khama was going to be their chief. How could his son, who would be half English, succeed him? To avoid trouble, the British rulers exiled Seretse Khama from Bechuanaland. He now says he will give up the Chieftainship. Ruth Khama is very happy to be returning to her adopted country.

STUDENTS STAGE FREEDOM MARCH

Nov 29, Barcelona, Spain   There have been student demonstrations in Spain. The students carried placards saying WE ARE AGAINST DICTATORSHIP – and below – FOR HUNGARY. They are really against General Franco's dictatorship in their own country. Everybody is under state control. Spaniards have to work harder than other Europeans for less pay. They cannot afford much to eat. They take great risks when they demonstrate against the state. Thousands of Spaniards have been imprisoned without trial.

CYPRUS LOSES ARCHBISHOP MAKARIOS

May 25, Nicosia   In March the British government deported Archbishop Makarios to the Seychelles, in the Indian Ocean. The British would like to give Cyprus self-government – but there must first be peace between Cypriot Greeks and Turks. Greece supports EOKA, the Greek nationalists' army; Turkey supports the Cypriot Turks. Greece and Turkey could go to war over who owns the island.

COUNTRIES BOYCOTT OLYMPICS

Dec 8, Melbourne, Australia   The Duke of Edinburgh opened the 16th Olympic Games – and the first to be held 'down under'. Several countries decided not to join in this year. They are protesting against Russia's invasion of Hungary, and Britain's and France's treatment of Egypt. But three African countries were represented for the first time: they are Kenya, Malawi and Ethiopia. Australian women performed well, though Britain's Judy Grinham won the 100m backstroke.

POWER FOR THE FUTURE

Oct 17, Cumbria   Britain's first nuclear power station was opened today by Her Majesty the Queen. It is at Calder Hall in Cumbria. It will provide electricity. Our usual sources of energy, coal and gas, may be finished within 200 years. It is therefore important to begin using other sources now.

Chris Brasher of Britain wins the 3000m Steeplechase.

Calder Hall nuclear power station in Cumbria

COLD WAR THAWS A LITTLE

April 26, London Mr. Khrushchev has been visiting Britain for talks with the Prime Minister, Sir Anthony Eden. Though the East and the West cannot agree, Mr. Khrushchev said, they could respect each other's point of view. There could be 'peaceful co-existence' between the two. This is seen as a softening of the Soviet hard-line policy toward the West. But in America, the Secretary of State said the United States must be prepared to go to the brink of war.

In February Mr. Khrushchev denounced Stalin. He said he was a brutal murderer. Perhaps people will be able to live happier lives now the truth is out. Some political prisoners have been freed.

Sir Anthony Eden (left) and Mr. Khrushchev shake hands at No. 10 Downing Street.

NEWS IN BRIEF . . .

ACTRESSES MARRY

June 29, Hollywood Today glamorous film star Marilyn Monroe married playwright Arthur Miller. His latest play, *The Crucible*, is about a witch-hunt in 17th-century America. It was first staged while Senator McCarthy was engaged on his modern witch-hunt of Communists. Marilyn will soon be off to London to film *The Prince and the Showgirl* with British actor Sir Lawrence Olivier.

In April, the beautiful American actress Grace Kelly married her Prince Charming. He is Prince Rainier of Monaco, a tiny country on the Mediterranean, between France and Italy. Grace's last film, *To Catch a Thief*, may have shown her a taste of the future. Its setting is the luxury French Riviera.

Wedding belles: Marilyn Monroe and husband Arthur Miller, above, and below, Grace Kelly, who is now Princess of Monaco.

NEW PLAY AT EDINBURGH FESTIVAL

Sept, Edinburgh One of Dylan Thomas's last works was a radio play called *Under Milk Wood*. It has now been made into a stage play. The play tells of a day in the life of a Welsh seaside village called Llaregub. It is full of comic, tender and sad characters and situations. It was first heard on the radio in 1954, narrated by Richard Burton. Just three months before, Dylan Thomas had died in New York.

FIGHT FOR FRENCH WOMEN'S RIGHTS

Oct 31, Grenoble, France A law passed 36 years ago makes family planning illegal in France. An enterprising woman is fighting the law. She has opened a birth-control clinic in Grenoble. Women have fewer rights in France than in England or America. A married woman even has to have her husband's permission to open a bank account.

1957

MIXED-RACE SCHOOLING RIOTS
SCHOOL ACCEPTS BLACK PUPILS

Sept 1, Little Rock, Arkansas   In the Southern states of America, blacks and whites have in the past attended different schools. This is changing in most states. But in Arkansas black and white children are not allowed to play games together – not even dominoes! Some teachers are speaking out against this law. In Little Rock, the school board has accepted nine black pupils for next term, three boys and six girls.

GOVERNOR SENDS IN THE GUARDS

Sept 2, Little Rock   The Governor of Arkansas surrounded Little Rock Central School with 270 National Guards today. Term begins tomorrow. The Governor says he wants to avoid trouble. But his action seems to invite a fight.

GUARDS REFUSE CHILDREN ENTRY

Sept 4, Little Rock   Two black and two white church leaders walked with the nine black pupils to school. The National Guard turned them away. So they walked back calmly and bravely through a huge mob of jeering whites. Americans in more liberal states are ashamed of the whites' behaviour.

National Guardsmen are posted outside this school at Little Rock on the Governor's orders.

PRESIDENT SENDS IN TROOPS

Sept 24, Little Rock   Yesterday the black students succeeded in entering Little Rock school. President Eisenhower has denounced the Governor of Arkansas. He has sent 1100 army paratroopers to Little Rock. He has also made the National Guard into a state police force. This means the Governor cannot give the Guard orders.

VICTORY HARD FOR BLACKS

Sept 30, Little Rock   The nine pupils are showing great courage. They are escorted to and from school by soldiers. Many of their schoolmates are unkind and insulting. But they are determined to stay. The Governor is furious, and many of his white voters are on his side. The fight for black rights in the south is not yet won.

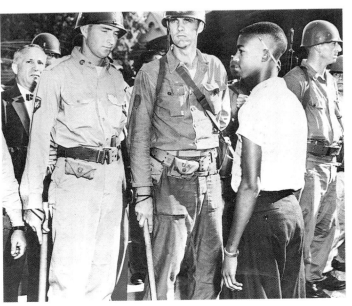

CONSERVATIVES LED BY MACMILLAN

Jan 10, London Sir Anthony Eden retired after the Suez crisis. Britain's new prime minister is Mr. Harold Macmillan. He backed Eden's policy in Suez. Now he will have to win the Americans round.

Conservative Prime Minister Mr. Harold Macmillan

SIX COUNTRIES IN ECONOMIC UNION

March 25, Rome Six Western nations today joined together to form a Common Market. The nations are France, West Germany, Italy, Belgium, Holland and Luxemburg. After the events in Hungary, they wish for a stronger central Europe. The six nations will allow their people to move freely between member countries. They will not tax each others' exports. Britain is not a member, though the six nations urged her to join them.

Laika is prepared for her space journey.

GOLD COAST BECOMES GHANA

March 7, Accra There were joyful celebrations in Accra tonight. The Gold Coast is the first British colony to become an independent member of the British Commonwealth. The new President, Dr. Kwame Nkrumah, renamed the country 'Ghana'. (A previous Ghana in West Africa was a wealthy trading nation in the 11th century.) As the British flag came down, the new Ghanaians hoisted their own flag of red, yellow and green.

Dr. Nkrumah in the Ghanaian Legislative Assembly

RUSSIAN SPACE SUCCESS

Nov 2, Moscow The Russians have launched the world's first artificial satellite. On October 4 an enormous rocket hurtled into space, carrying a sphere which is now circling the earth. It is called *Sputnik I*, and it weighs 83 kg (182 lb).

Now the Russians have put a much larger satellite, *Sputnik II*, into orbit. It is circling the earth at about 28,800 km an hour – with a dog called Laika on board. Laika is in a sealed container. She receives food at regular intervals. Machines record the effects of space travel on a living animal. Other instruments are measuring the sun's radiation, and sending signals back to earth. These signals have been picked up in many parts of the world.

Western scientists are amazed that such a large satellite could be sent into orbit. It weighs over 500 kg (half a ton).

NEWS IN BRIEF . . .

AMERICAN GIRL MAKES HISTORY

July 6, Wimbledon Althea Gibson's life has been made up of tennis 'firsts'. She was born 30 years ago in Harlem, New York. In 1950 she was the first black competitor in a tennis tournament at Forest Hills, in the United States. She was the first black lady to win Wimbledon doubles, the French singles and doubles, and the Italian singles. And she has crowned her career this week by winning both the singles and doubles championships at Wimbledon.

Miss Gibson, the number one seed at Wimbledon

THE BEAT GENERATION

June 2, San Francisco 'Beatniks' in khaki trousers, sandals and sweaters are the in-crowd in America. The men wear beards and the girls use heavy eyeshadow. Sometimes they smoke 'pot', but they don't go in for hard drugs. They see their way of life as a new religion. They say they love everybody and everything. Their talk is full of slang: 'chicks', 'dig', 'bread'. The word 'like' occurs in almost every sentence: 'Like it means nothing'; 'It's like cool'.

THE CONSUMER SOCIETY IS HERE

July 20, Britain "Most of our people have never had it so good", Mr. Harold Macmillan has said. Our parents and grandparents would be astonished to see our houses today. Washing machines, telephones, radios and refrigerators were real luxuries in the 1930s. The state looks after us better. We have sickness benefits, family allowances, and pensions.

RACING DRIVER BEATS OWN RECORD

August 4, Germany Juan Fangio has become the world car-racing champion by winning the German Grand Prix which is the toughest circuit in Europe. On the bumpy track tyres burst, mirrors fall off, and shock-absorbers become red hot. Last year Fangio drove a record lap in 9 minutes 41.6 seconds in a Lancia Ferrari. In this year's race, in a Maserati, his fastest lap was 9 minutes 17.4 seconds. Afterwards Fangio said, "I took myself and my car to the limit, and perhaps a little bit more."

SPACE EXPLORATION AND ENTERTAINMENT

Sept 26, London and New York Are we all space mad? Film-makers seem to think so. We have an endless diet of science fiction, evil aliens, mad scientists, shock and horror. The latest is *The Incredible Shrinking Man*. It follows *Invaders from Mars* and *Invasion of the Body Snatchers*.

West Side Story, a musical now showing in New York, brings us back to earth, and to the present. This is the story of a modern Romeo and Juliet. Leonard Bernstein's marvellous music accompanies teenage gang warfare and a haunting love story.

A scene from *West Side Story*

BRITONS DISCOVER COSTA DEL SOL

July 15, Madrid, Spain Tourism is a new industry in Spain. The Spaniards did not like it at first. Many of them are poor, and resent serving well-off holiday-makers. But tourists bring money to the country. Plots of land on the unspoiled Costa Brava are selling well. The rate of exchange is very much in the tourists' favour, making food and drink there very cheap.

1958

CIVIL WAR IN ALGERIA

ALGERIANS WANT SELF-GOVERNMENT

Jan 1, Algiers   Algeria has been a French colony for a hundred years. It has a million French settlers. Most native Algerians are Muslims. Many have to migrate to France to find work. There is none for them in Algeria.

Members of a political party, the National Liberation Front (FLN), want to get rid of the French settlers. They want self-government. For four years they have been fighting the French army and the settlers.

ALGERIA TO STAY FRENCH

Feb 5, Paris   The French parliament has voted for Algeria to remain a part of the French republic. They say that both Frenchmen and Algerian Muslims should take part in the Algerian government. The FLN are totally against this. They continue to fight for independence.

ATROCITIES IN NORTH AFRICA

Feb 12, Algiers   The Prime Minister of neighbouring Tunisia has asked French troops to leave Algeria. The French have bombed a Tunisian village just over the border. They thought FLN fighters were hiding there. The bombs killed and wounded 75 Tunisians, many of them children.

FRENCH SETTLERS SHOW STRENGTH

May 13, Algiers   There are now 500,000 French soldiers in Algeria. In the guerrilla fighting, casualties on both sides have been heavy. The army and the settlers are afraid that the French government will give in to the FLN. So today they seized government buildings, and business has come to a standstill. In Paris, people have been rioting in support of the settlers.

The French government is weak, and the war in Algeria is costing France more than it can afford. The settlers want General de Gaulle to take over. They are sure he would support them.

French troops near Algiers display the stock of arms seized in a recent battle with FLN fighters, 44 of whom were killed.

DE GAULLE SPEAKS TO ALGERIA

Oct 23, Paris General de Gaulle became Premier of France in June. He has dashed the settlers' hopes of a French Algeria. He wants the country to be self-supporting, but with strong ties to France. He will see that 400,000 jobs are created for Algerians.

MANCHESTER LOSES HALF ITS TEAM

Feb 6, Munich, Germany A horrific aircrash here today has killed seven members of Manchester United football team. They were on their way home from a match in Belgrade. The plane hit a fence and crashed into an airport building. Several journalists were also killed, and the team manager is badly hurt. The news has shocked the people of Manchester. The team would have played in the Cup Final in May.

The crashed Elizabethan aircraft at Munich airport, with snow still falling

NOBEL WINNER DENIED PRIZE

Dec 10, Stockholm, Sweden Boris Pasternak has been awarded the Nobel Prize for Literature. His most recent book is *Dr Zhivago*. He could only publish it abroad, because of Russian censorship. The government of the USSR has banned his work and will not allow him to accept the prize.

MARCH AGAINST NUCLEAR WEAPONS

April 7, Aldermaston The new Campaign for Nuclear Disarmament (CND) received publicity today when a crowd of 3000 arrived here from London. Many had walked all the way. Scientists at Aldermaston are developing new types of nuclear weapons. CND believes that the arms race is no way to ensure peace. The president of CND is the famous philosopher and writer, Bertrand Russell.

Demonstrators against the H-bomb march on Whitehall.

NEW SPACE AGENCY OPENED

July 29, Washington The Americans want to catch up with the Russians in space exploration. The National Aeronautics and Space Agency (NASA) has been opened. It will carry out research on rockets and space craft. The US has two satellites in a higher orbit than that of the Russian Sputniks. One of them is making its own electricity from sunlight. They are small satellites, and their purpose is to record data about the earth and space.

MIDDLE EASTERN CRISIS ALARMS WEST

July 14, Baghdad, Iraq Earlier this year Egypt and Syria became the United Arab Republic (UAR). Iraq and Jordan also united their two kingdoms. Now there has been a coup in Iraq. The 23-year-old King Feisal, his uncle, and his Prime Minister have all been murdered. Colonel Nasser of Egypt has backed the coup. King Hussein of Jordan is now afraid that the UAR, led by Nasser, may attack Jordan. The British and Americans are landing troops in Jordan. The Russians back the UAR. The two superpowers, America and the Soviet Union, are on opposite sides of a dangerous international conflict once again.

POPE WINS PRISONERS' FREEDOM

Nov 7, Barcelona Three days ago the new pope, John XXIII, was crowned in Rome. Spain's General Franco announced that in honour of the occasion political prisoners would be released. Today over 16,000 men and women were set free and have joined their families. Many were imprisoned without trial, and on minor charges. There is no sign that General Franco's government will change its policy.

His Holiness Pope John XXIII

KHRUSHCHEV WANTS BERLIN FREE

Nov 30, Moscow Mr. Khrushchev has got rid of all his rivals in the Kremlin. He is now looking towards East Germany. He says Berlin should be a 'free city'. West Berliners dread this possibility. The city, they say, would not be free for very long. The French, British and Americans are refusing to leave their zones of Berlin. Berlin is still an escape route for East Germans. Nearly a million have left the Communist East since 1952.

ELVIS HAS HIS MARCHING ORDERS

Mar 24, New York Elvis Presley has been called up for his compulsory military service. The king of rock and roll has had his hair cut short. He can no longer wear the pink jackets and eye make-up that drive the girls wild. Friends say Elvis is just a quiet and polite country lad. He is also big business: his fans buy his records in millions.

Elvis Presley, the rock 'n roll star

NEWS IN BRIEF . . .

JET PLANES CARRY PASSENGERS

Oct 4, London Today the first passengers flew from London to New York in a jet plane, BOAC's Comet. Pan American plans to start a jet service with Boeing 707s before the end of the month. Up to now, most travellers between the two countries have sailed on luxury ocean-going liners. These famous ships may go out of business as air travel becomes faster.

Passengers enjoy luxury aboard the tourist cabin of a Comet.

CIRCLING IS GOOD FOR THE HIPS

Sept 30, London The latest craze to reach Europe from the United States is the hula-hoop. Spinning for health, for pleasure, to music, for the *Guinness Book of Records* – whatever people twirl the hoop for it is selling millions of these plastic rings.

In Paris's Champs-Elysées traffic came to a standstill when girls demonstrated the hula-hoop. They were dressed in bathing suits and accompanied by a Country and Western band!

THE LAST CURTSEYS

March 18, London Today the last débutantes were presented to the Queen. Every year 'debs' have made their curtseys at Court at the start of the social season in London, where these young ladies 'come out'. Nowadays this practice seems old-fashioned, and this year's crop of débutantes will be the last.

The tradition was also seen as taking up too much of Her Majesty's valuable time.

BEEHIVE HAIRSTYLES STAY PUT

Nov 30, London Girls are back-combing their hair and holding it high off the forehead with plenty of hairspray. The 'beehive' hair-do stays put! This style goes with pretty print dresses and high-heeled shoes.

HOW LONG DO WE LIVE?

Dec 31, London People can expect to live longer now than they did 18 years ago. In 1938 a man lived on average 58½ years, and a woman 63 years. Today the averages are 67½ years for a man, and 74 years for a woman.

1959

HEADING FOR SPACE
LUNA II SPEEDS TO THE SUN

Jan 12, Moscow   The Russians have launched a rocket called *Luna II* towards the sun. It is the first rocket to escape earth's gravity. It will not return to the earth, but for some time it will send signals and information back.

NASA IS TRAINING ASTRONAUTS

May 28, Washington   NASA is training seven men for the exciting but frightening task of being sent into space. The men will be called 'astronauts'. In specially designed chambers they are finding out what it is like to be weightless. They will not be sent into space until more tests are made with animal passengers. Today two monkeys returned safely after a 480-km (300-mile) journey into space.

ANOTHER 'FIRST' FOR USSR

Oct 27, Moscow   This evening viewers of Moscow television saw the first extraordinary pictures of the other side of the moon – the side we never see. A Russian satellite, *Luna III*, was launched on October 4. Two days later it began to orbit the moon. A camera on the satellite took pictures for 40 minutes, and transmitted them to earth. Many of these pictures have been printed in the world's newspapers today. Russian scientists have already named eight features on the moon's far side.

DALAI LAMA SAFE IN INDIA

April 19, Lhasa, Tibet   The Buddhist ruler of Tibet, the Dalai Lama, has been forced to leave his capital city, Lhasa, in disguise. When the Chinese marched into Tibet they promised to modernize the country, then leave. That was nine years ago, and they are still here. They have ruled the Tibetans harshly. Tibetan guerrillas are fighting the Chinese in the east. They have blown up bridges and mined roads. Chinese soldiers were told to capture the Dalai Lama dead or alive, but they were too late. He has arrived safely in India. His successor, the Panchen Lama, has agreed to co-operate with the Chinese.

The disguised Dalai Lama escapes from Tibet in the dark robes of a servant.

CUBA FREED FROM DICTATOR
REJOICING IN HAVANA

Jan 2, Havana, Cuba There has been a coup in Cuba, and President Batista has fled to the Dominican Republic. He has ruled Cuba, an island in Central America, as the cruel dictator of a police state for many years. Since he came to power the rich have become richer. Havana is full of Cadillacs, luxury houses and gambling casinos. But most Cubans are penniless and many are starving. There are few jobs, no unemployment benefits, and no health care.

The coup was led by a young lawyer, Fidel Castro. He rode into Havana yesterday on a tank. His second-in-command is an Argentinian doctor, Che Guevara. In 1956 they began their guerrilla attacks from the mountains. In 2½ years their small band of adventurers has become a national movement. There was great rejoicing all over Cuba today that Batista's rule has ended.

Fidel Castro, the leader of the coup in Cuba

CASTRO WELCOMED IN WASHINGTON

April 15, Washington Fidel Castro has been given a great welcome on his arrival for talks with the Vice-President. The United States is pleased that he will hold free elections in Cuba. Castro was sworn in as Prime Minister in February. Manuel Urrutia is the President.

THE US THINKS AGAIN

July 18, Havana The United States is now worried that Castro is going too far. He has dismissed Urrutia and made himself President of Cuba. He is dividing large sugar estates and distributing the land to Cuban farmers. Many of these estates belong to Americans. The United States has controlled Cuba's economy in the past, importing two-thirds of Cuba's sugar at fixed prices. Castro seems to be moving towards Communism. He is also executing Batista's supporters after speedy trials.

MORE TROUBLE IN VIETNAM

July 9, Saigon, South Vietnam Communists in South Vietnam have rebelled against the republican government. They are supported by the Viet Cong (forces of the Viet Minh) in North Vietnam. Today they killed two American soldiers. The South Vietnamese army is being trained by the United States.

PEACE IN SIGHT FOR CYPRUS

Dec 14, Nicosia Both Greeks and Turks in Cyprus are hoping for peace at last. The British are leaving the country. They have allowed Archbishop Makarios to return from exile, and today he has become President of a new independent Cyprus. His Vice-President is Turkish. Colonel Grivas has disbanded EOKA and left for Greece. After four years of bitter fighting both sides pray that Greeks and Turks will be able to forget their differences and live peacefully together.

KHRUSHCHEV MEETS EISENHOWER

Sept 20, Los Angeles Five days ago Mr. Khrushchev stepped out of his Russian plane, the most advanced jet the Americans had ever seen. He is visiting the United States for two weeks. In Washington he presented President Eisenhower with a model of a rocket. The real rocket had landed on the moon only a few hours earlier. The American President was a little taken aback by this reminder of the Russians' success in space!

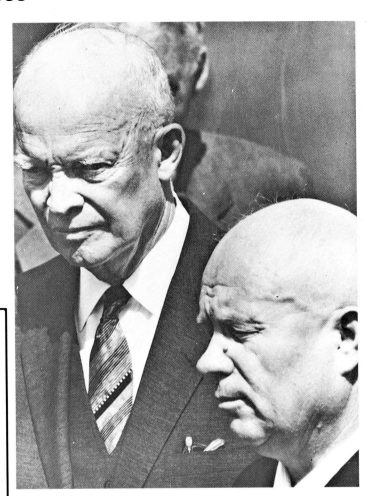

Russian leader Nikita Khrushchev with US President Eisenhower (left), during Mr. Khrushchev's visit

KENYA'S EMERGENCY ENDS

Nov 10, Nairobi The Mau Mau rebellion is over. Hundreds of forest fighters have been captured. About 10,000 Mau Mau have been killed. They in turn killed about 2000 Kikuyu civilians, 1000 government troops, and 58 Europeans and Asians. The land question, which started the terrorist attacks, is being looked into by the government.

NEWS IN BRIEF . . .

'THE BRAIN' WAS CHEATING

Nov 2, New York Charles Van Doren will resign from his teaching job at Colombia University. This handsome and popular man has admitted that he won $129,000 dishonestly. In the TV quiz show, 'Twenty-One', he answered the hardest questions, week after week. He was as popular as a film star all over America. But one of his rivals spilt the beans. The most popular quiz competitors were shown the answers in advance. Other competitors who were shown the answers include an 11-year-old girl who won $32,000.

YOUNG PEOPLE WITH MONEY TO SPEND HELP THE ECONOMY

Nov 8, London The economy is booming. Teenagers have more money than ever before. They are buying soft drinks, fast food, clothes and records. Sales of 7-Up, Pepsi and Coke have soared. Because pop music is so popular, 70 per cent of all records are bought by teenagers. Many people in their twenties can afford the new Minis. These little cars are cheap and reliable. With more people driving, more roads have to be built. Britain's first motorway, the M1, was opened this week.

The new M1 motorway being swept ready for opening

PEOPLE OF THE FIFTIES

Sir Anthony Eden, British politician 1897–1977

Anthony Eden was born in the north of England. He was a gifted linguist, and studied Arabic and Persian. He was elected as a Conservative MP in 1923. He was Foreign Secretary when Hitler invaded Austria in 1938. He resigned because he did not agree with the way Neville Chamberlain gave in to Hitler. Later he became Foreign Secretary twice more, and Prime Minister in 1955. Eden welcomed Khrushchev to London in 1953, to try to ease the East-West tension. He helped to solve an oil dispute in Iran in 1954. He was responsible for establishing SEATO. Eden was much criticized for the warlike way in which Britain handled the Suez crisis. This led to his resignation as Prime Minister on January 9 1957. In 1961 he became the Earl of Avon.

Sir Stanley Matthews, footballer 1915-

Outside-right Stanley Matthews is said to have been the greatest dribbler of all time. Certainly he showed his great talent in the FA Cup Final of 1953. He began his career in 1931, playing for Stoke City and later Blackpool. His first international match was in 1938, and over the years he played in 53 more.

In the New Year's Honours List of 1965 he was made a Knight – the first footballer to be called 'Sir'. Shortly afterwards, at the age of 50, he gave up his footballing career.

Agatha Christie, novelist 1890-1976

Dame Agatha Christie will be remembered for a very long time because of the two characters she created: Hercule Poirot, and Miss Jane Marple. They appeared in dozens of her detective novels. Agatha Christie's play *The Mousetrap* was on stage continuously for 40 years. *Murder on the Orient Express* and *Death on the Nile* have each been filmed twice.

After her marriage to Colonel Christie ended in divorce, in 1930 she married a distinguished archaeologist, Max Mallowan. She became a Dame of the British Empire in 1971.

Jomo Kenyatta, Kenyan politician 1894-1978

His real name was Kamau wa Ngengi. He grew up in a Kikuyu village, at the time when the British started to colonize Kenya. He went to a mission school, and could speak English well. He spent two years in Moscow, and 20 years in London. He studied anthropology, and wrote a book about the Kikuyu people, *Facing Mount Kenya*.

In 1946 he returned to Kenya, and became head of the Kenya African Union. He was a very powerful speaker. He wanted Africans to have equal opportunities with whites. In 1953 the British accused him of leading Mau Mau. He was imprisoned for nine years. In 1964 he became President of an independent Kenya. He was immensely popular. Everyone called him 'Mzee' (Elder, or Old One). Under his Presidency Kenya had a free press, and good health and education services.

Eva (Evita) Perón 1919-52

Eva Perón was born in a tiny village, but grew to be the most influential person in Argentina. She was an actress before she married Juan Perón in 1945. She campaigned tirelessly for her husband, especially among the poorer people. With the money she raised, Eva Perón was able to increase workers' pay, and open hundreds of new schools and hospitals. In 1949 Eva Perón formed a feminist movement, and persuaded her husband to change the law so as to allow women to vote. She fell ill, and three years later died of cancer. The people of Argentina mourned in their thousands. They called her a saint.

Elvis Presley, American singer 1935-77

Elvis grew up in the Southern state of Mississippi. He often heard 'blues' music sung by black singers, and he imitated them. One day in 1954, a recording company wanted to engage a white singer who could sound like a black singer. Elvis was exactly what they were looking for. Two years later he released 'Heartbreak Hotel', the first of 45 recordings that sold over a million copies. Elvis changed the whole art of pop singing by his personality. After two years in the army he was back in show business, but the strain was beginning to tell. He put on weight, and took drugs. He died in the huge house he had bought in Memphis, Tennessee.

Grace Kelly (Princess Grace of Monaco) 1929-82

Grace Kelly was born in Philadelphia, USA. When her schooldays were over she studied drama, and was soon playing in films opposite well-known actors, including Gary Cooper and Clark Gable. When she played Bing Crosby's wife in *Country Girl* (1954), she received an Academy Award for best actress. The great Alfred Hitchcock chose her to be his leading lady in *Dial M for Murder* (1954), and *To Catch a Thief* (1955). He said she had the elegance and appeal he wanted.

On April 19 1956 her life changed. She married the ruler of the little state of Monaco, Prince Rainier II. They had three children. Her death was quite unexpected. She was driving with her younger daughter on a winding hilly road in the south of France. She had a stroke, and the car went out of control. It plunged down an embankment. Her daughter survived the crash.

Ernesto Guevara de la Serna (Che Guevara) 1928-67

'Che' Guevara was an Argentinian, an athlete, a scholar, and a medical doctor. But he devoted his life to fighting corrupt regimes. He felt that people in underdeveloped countries should struggle to be free of dictatorship and poverty. He met Fidel Castro in Mexico, and together they went to Cuba. They led the guerrillas against Batista's government. Che Guevara became a Cuban citizen when Castro took power, and served in his government. In the 1960s he joined Patrice Lumumba's national movement in the Congo (Central Africa). When that failed he became a guerrilla leader in Bolivia (South America). In 1967 he was captured by government forces there, and shot.

For the first time ever

1950	USA	Photocopier machines available
		Pre-recorded tapes produced
	UK	A company starts to sell air charter holidays
		Schools start 'O' and 'A' level exams
1951	W. Germany	Long-playing records on sale
	USA	Atomic energy produces electric power
		Experiments with colour TV are successful
	UK	A supermarket is opened
		Zebra crossings come into use
		Cities experiment with adventure playgrounds
1952	USA	A heart pacemaker is fitted
		Video recorders are on sale
		Painting-by-numbers kits on sale
	UK	Tea is sold in tea-bags
1953	UK	Successful open-heart operation
		The Samaritans established
	Germany	A fan heater is marketed
	USA	Music synthesizers invented
1954	USSR	An atomic power station opened
	USA	A vaccine for polio is developed
		TV dinners are advertised
	UK	First comprehensive school
		The government introduces VAT
		A supersonic fighter plane flies
1955	USA	Tranquillizers are in general use
		Transistors are used in radios
	UK	Firms issue luncheon vouchers
		A Wimpy bar is opened
		Bird's Eye package fish fingers
	France	Non-stick saucepans on sale
1956	Switzerland	A Eurovision song contest is held
	USA	Go-karts become popular
	UK	The government launches Premium Bonds
		Wall cracks can be filled with Polyfilla

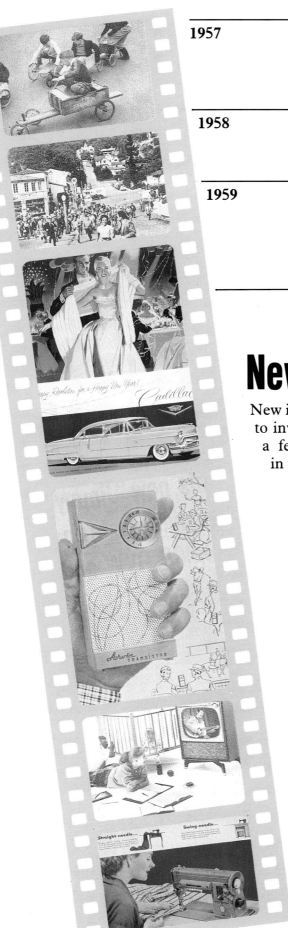

1957	USA	Portable electric typewriters on sale
		Frisbies are all the rage
	UK	Microwave ovens on sale
	Japan	Transistor radios produced
1958	UK	A planetarium is opened
	USA	Windsurfing becomes popular
		Stereo records are on sale
1959	USA	Transistors used in computers
		Identikit used
	UK	A trial post-code is used
		A walk is organized for charity
		A drive-in bank opens

New words and expressions

New inventions, and new habits and occupations, cause people to invent new words. They also invent new slang. These are a few of the words and phrases used for the first time in the 1950s in England and America.

astronaut	fall-out
bathyscaphe	hippy
best-seller	leisure clothing
bikini	a mobile
brand image	neat (slang)
brinkmanship	pesticide
the buck stops here!	sputnik
cinerama	square (slang)
cool (slang)	teddy boy
to dig (somebody,	terylene
something)	video
disincentive	
egg-head	

How many of these words and expressions do we still use today? Do you know what they all mean?

Glossary

abdicate: to give up the throne

abduct: to kidnap

anthropology: the study of human beings

archaeology: the study of the past, usually by digging up objects buried in the ground

asthma: a disease which causes difficulties in breathing

asset: something or someone useful, worth having

become extinct: die out for ever

BOAC: British Overseas Airways Corporation (now part of BA)

call-up: notice to serve in the armed forces.

to campaign: to make the public interested in something, often an election

casual labour: workers who are hired for a short time; seasonal employment

coexistence: living together

compulsory: forced; something you are made to do

corrupt: acting unlawfully, often to gain money

Cypriot: a native of Cyprus

denounce: accuse, disagree with officially

depose: remove from the throne

fossil: remains of an animal or plant that has been preserved, and is still recognizable

guerrilla fighters: people who fight independently; not in the regular army

Kremlin: fortified part of a Russian town; in this case, the place in Moscow where the government sits

at loggerheads: disagreeing strongly

lottery: a raffle organized by the state to raise money

memento: something you keep in order to remember someone, or some occasion

mudflat: stretch of mud by river or sea, uncovered at low tide

nuclear scientist: someone working on atomic projects

oath: a solemn promise

orbit: the path of a satellite round a planet

pact: agreement, treaty

paratroops: soldiers who are dropped by parachute

philosopher: a person who studies knowledge, wisdom

pilgrim: a person who makes a special journey to a religious place

pseudo-: false, pretending

radioactive: atomic explosions cause 'radioactivity', or a change in the structure of a cell. If cells in a human body are affected, the person becomes permanently ill

satellite: a natural or artificial object that goes round the earth – the moon is a natural satellite

stratosphere: layer of air high above the earth

USSR/Soviet Union: these names refer to the same country

veto: forbid, reject

vaccine: a liquid used to inject people as a protection from disease. The vaccine is usually a mild form of the disease itself

Further reading

Post War World series; *USA since 1945*: Elizabeth Campling. Batsford 1988

Post War World series; *USSR since 1945*: Elizabeth Campling. Batsford 1990

Portrait of a Decade series; *The 1950s*: Nance Lui Fyson. Batsford 1989

Living through History series; *Britain in the 1950s*: Monica Hodgson. Batsford 1989

Finding out about life in Britain in 1950s: Sarah Harris. Batsford 1985

Fashions of a decade: 1950s: Jacqueline Herald. Batsford 1991

The Twentieth Century: R. J. Unstead. A. & C. Black 1974

How we used to live 1954–1970: Freda Kelsall. A. & C. Black 1987

The Fifties: Neil Thomson. Franklin Watts 1991

The Fifties: Tom Stacy. Wayland 1989

The Forties and Fifties: Nathaniel Harris. Macdonald Educational 1985

CONTENTS

Author:
Fiona Macdonald studied History at Cambridge University and at the University of East Anglia. She has taught in schools, adult education, university, and is the author of numerous books for children on historical topics.

Artist:
Mark Bergin was born in Hastings in 1961. He studied at Eastbourne College of Art and has illustrated many children's non-fiction books. He is especially interested in military history. He lives in Bexhill-on-Sea with his wife and three children.

Additional artists: Mark Peppé and Gerald Wood

Series designer and creator: David Salariya

Editor: Karen Barker Smith

Assistant Editor: Michael Ford

Published in Great Britain in 2003 by
Book House, an imprint of
The Salariya Book Company Ltd
25 Marlborough Place, Brighton BN1 1UB

Please visit the Salariya Book Company at:
www.salariya.com
www.book-house.co.uk

ISBN 1 904194 73 7

A catalogue record for this book is available from the British Library.

Printed and bound in Belgium.
Printed on paper from sustainable forests.

Photographic credits
t=top b=bottom c=centre l=left r=right

The Art Archive/ Archeological Museum Madrid/ Dagli Orti: 6bl
The Art Archive/ Bibliothèque Nationale, Paris/ The Art Archive: 13r
The Art Archive/ Museo Etnografico, Palemo/ Dagli Orti: 21
The Art Archive/ Musée de la Tapisserie Bayeux/ Dagli Orti: 10/11t
The Art Archive/ British Library/ British Library: 33
Bibliothèque Nationale, Paris/ Bridgeman Art Library: 15, 34
The Board of Trustees of the Armouries: 17, 25
Bridgeman Art Library: 22, 28, 31, 41
Bridgeman Giraudon/ Lauros: 37
Jeffrey L Thomas: 11b
John Foxx Images: 12b
Kunsthistorisches Museum, Wien: 23
Lauros-Giraudon/ Bridgeman Art Library: 20
Mark Bergin: 26/27
The Pierpont Morgan Library/ Art Resource, NY: 35

Every effort has been made to trace copyright holders. The Salariya Book Co. apologises for any unintentional omissions and would be pleased, in such cases, to add an acknowledgement in future editions.

BATTLE ZONES

Warfare in the Middle Ages

Written by
Fiona Macdonald

Illustrated by
Mark Bergin

BOOK HOUSE

THE MEDIEVAL WORLD

The years from around AD 1000 to AD 1500 are often called the Middle Ages or the medieval period. During that time a splendid civilisation developed in Europe. It combined the laws and customs of many different peoples – Romans, Celts, Angles, Saxons, Franks, Slavs and Vikings – with ideas based on the teachings of the Roman Catholic Church. European peoples lived in many different states, ruled by kings, princes and noblemen. Each state was fiercely independent, but rulers often made friendly alliances with foreign countries to help defend their own kingdoms or to fight a shared enemy. Merchants, scholars and religious pilgrims also travelled long distances to meet and work peacefully with men and women in other European lands.

However, the peoples of medieval Europe also made contact through war, fighting against neighbouring states or fighting their own countrymen in civil wars. They also battled against enemies along European frontiers. These included pagan tribes in Russia, Ottoman Turks in the Balkans, and Muslim princes in North Africa and the Middle East.

Romanesque processional cross made of ivory, 1063

Europe

North Atlantic Ocean

Wars the R

SPAIN

MULTICULTURAL SOCIETIES

Most Europeans were Christians and the Roman Catholic Church was immensely rich and powerful. It owned vast amounts of land together with religious treasures such as beautifully-illustrated manuscripts and this processional cross (left). Priests and monks were the most well-educated people in Europe and held most of the prominent positions in governments and universities. But there was also a rich and cultured Muslim civilisation in southern Spain and Jewish communities lived in many European towns.

SCANDINAVIA

Baltic Sea

Crusades against pagan peoples

Moscow

Mongol invaders

Joan of Arc burnt, 1431

Vienna

Slav kingdoms

Ottoman Turks conquer Serbia, 1389

Fall of Constantinople, 1453

Genoa

Venice

Black Sea

Mediterranean Sea

SICILY

TURKEY

Crusader

CA

Jerusalem

7

MEDIEVAL SOCIETY

edieval society was based on war, and war-leaders such as kings and nobles were the richest and most powerful people. Their main duty was to fight bravely, however dangerous this might be. As one early-medieval poet explained, "A king is for glory, not for long life". They were supported by loyal knights. In return, kings gave knights land and important roles such as officers in royal armies.

CASTLES AND COTTAGES
Huge stone castles towered over churches and other buildings. Peasants lived in small, wood-and-plaster cottages. In wartime, priests and peasants sought refuge inside the castle.

STRUCTURE OF MEDIEVAL SOCIETY
Most medieval people were peasant farmers. Free men and women often lived in towns, where they made goods or traded. Knights might own estates, or rely on their fighting skills for a living. Nobles were related to royalty or royal advisors.

King
Church
Nobles
Knights
Peasants

Kings, nobles and knights were responsible for maintaining law and order. They held courts for the peasants living on their land and took part in parliaments which made laws and raised taxes.

Throughout Christian Europe, leaders had a duty to defend the Catholic Church. In return, powerful Church officials helped run their governments and gave them moral, spiritual and political support, while priests, monks and nuns prayed for their souls. Some Church leaders encouraged Christian soldiers to fight against all non-Christians. Others urged warriors to fight only 'just' (fair) wars, in defence of themselves and their country.

LOYAL KNIGHTS

At the end of their training new knights swore an oath of 'fealty', or loyalty, to the king. Kings gave knights land to farm and allowed them to build castles. In return, knights agreed to fight for the king, or to pay a tax called 'scutage' (shield-money) if they did not fight. A knight's equipment was expensive and some young noblemen tried to avoid becoming knights because they could not afford it.

RENTS AND TAXES

Landowners collected money from the people living on their lands and demanded fines from anyone who broke the law. Peasants 'belonged' to the lord and could not change jobs, move house or marry without his permission. Lords could also force peasant men to join their armies.

INVADERS

Throughout the Middle Ages, land was the main source of wealth and power. It is not surprising that it was also the cause of most medieval wars. In the early Middle Ages, war-leaders won fame and praise by raiding and plundering new territory. Towards the end of the medieval era, such leaders fought to defend their countries from foreign enemies. As invading armies advanced into enemy territory, they built forts and camps for shelter and protection. Later, victorious kings built castles as bases for army commanders, government officials, clerks, servants and all the troops they needed to keep control of conquered lands.

THE BAYEUX TAPESTRY (above) This tapestry is a length of embroidery almost 70 m long that tells the story of the Norman invasion in picture-strip form. It was made soon after the conquest by French noblewomen and nuns.

CONQUERORS

In 1066, the ambitious Duke William of Normandy (a state in northern France) invaded England and defeated English King Harold at the Battle of Hastings. William took land and treasures away from English nobles and gave them to his own knights. He introduced the French language, Norman customs and Norman laws.

Helmet

Sword

Shield

Chain mail

NORMAN ARMOUR

A Norman knight (right) wore a metal helmet, with an extra strip of metal to protect his nose. He had a chain mail shirt and was armed with a sword and shield.

At other times, rulers of rich, powerful states took over smaller, weaker kingdoms nearby. For example, during the 13th and 14th centuries, kings of England fought many wars to conquer and control their less powerful neighbours, the Welsh and the Scots.

Edward I of England (ruled 1272-1307) was a ruthless warrior. From 1276 to 1283 he fought successfully to conquer Wales. In 1296 he invaded Scotland. Although he won many victories, earning the nickname 'Hammer of the Scots', he never managed to control Scotland.

Illustration of Edward I, shown here in Parliament with King Alexander III of Scotland and Prince Llewellyn of Wales.

Caerphilly Castle (below), in Wales, was built between 1268 and 1271 by a supporter of King Edward I in his fight to conquer all Wales. Caerphilly is the largest Welsh castle ever built. It was designed as a 'concentric' castle, with two sets of walls, one inside the other. The inner walls were higher than the outer ones, allowing two teams to defend it.

LOCAL HERO
Robert Bruce (left, ruled 1306-1329) led the Scottish fight against English invaders. At first defeated, he made raids on English armies and captured English-held castles. In 1314 he defeated the English at the Battle of Bannockburn. This was the only time an English army led by an English king was defeated in Scotland. Bruce himself was brave and very lucky, but the rest of his family was not so fortunate. Three of his brothers and three brothers-in-law were captured by the English and killed.

CRUSADERS

In 1095, Alexius I, ruler of the Byzantine Empire, wrote to Pope Urban II, head of the Catholic Church in Rome. Alexius asked fellow Christians for help in defending his lands against the Seljuk Turks, Muslim tribesmen who were attacking from the East. Urban preached a rousing sermon, calling on all Christian kings to help Alexius. He also urged them to fight against Muslim sultans (princes) who ruled the 'Holy Land' – the territory around the city of Jerusalem (now in Israel). Pope Urban's call to arms started a series of wars between Christians and Muslims that lasted from 1096 to 1291. They were called the 'Crusades' after the Latin word for cross ('crux'). Although soldiers on both sides fought bravely for their beliefs, the Crusades left a heritage of mistrust and bitterness that continues today.

HOLY WARRIOR
Louis IX of France (below) was made a saint for his religious zeal – not for his fighting skills!

He set off for the Holy Land in 1248 and after years of unsuccessful fighting, he was captured by Egyptian troops in 1254. He was ransomed and returned to France, but left for the Crusades again in 1270. He died of plague the next year, in Tunis, North Africa.

HOLY SITE
The Dome of the Rock (left) is a beautiful mosque in Jerusalem. It was built in the 7th century and like the city itself, has been sacred to Jews, Christians and Muslims.

SUCCESS – AND FAILURE!

During the First Crusade Christian armies surrounded the Muslim city of Antioch in Syria (right). They besieged it for seven and a half months. But Antioch was well-defended, with 450 watchtowers and well-stocked with food. Eventually, the Crusaders persuaded a Turkish guard to surrender one of the towers and they captured the city in a night-time assault. But the very next day, a Muslim army arrived and trapped the besiegers inside the city they had just taken. Many of them died from plague and famine.

CRUSADER KNIGHT, C. 1250

A Crusader knight (below) wore a complete suit of chain mail, with a heavy great helm to protect his head. He carried a long lance, used to stab an enemy, or knock him off his horse. He wore a surcoat over his chain mail, decorated with the Christian cross. Foot soldiers (kneeling, front) wore tunics of padded cloth and round kettle helmets. They were armed with a deadly new weapon – the crossbow.

The capture of Antioch in 1098, shown on a 15th-century French manuscript

Great helm

Lance

Surcoat

Kettle helmet

Crossbow

DEFENDERS

In 1206, in Mongolia, a young prince named Temujin was proclaimed 'Genghis Khan' (supreme ruler) and set out to conquer the world. For the rest of the 13th century, the Christian peoples of Europe and the Muslim peoples of the Middle East had to defend themselves against Mongol invasions. The Mongols were nomads, who roamed across the wide steppes of Central Asia, seeking food and water for their animals. They were divided into separate tribes, who fought among themselves. By uniting the Mongols and showing them what they could plunder from the rich lands all around them, Genghis Khan made them much more dangerous than ever before.

WARRIORS ON HORSEBACK
Mongols fought on horseback, so they could advance more quickly than armies of foot soldiers. They could also stage quick 'hit and run' raids on enemies, turning in their saddles to fire backwards as they galloped to safety. Their favourite weapons were short, curved bows that fired deadly arrows. They wore armour made of small metal plates, fastened to leather tunics, and pointed metal helmets.

NOMAD LIFE

Mongols lived in large domed tents, called 'gers'. They were made of felt (boiled wool) stretched over a collapsible wooden frame. Inside each tent, the floor was covered by rugs. To combat the icy Mongolian winter, a fire was kept burning constantly. One side of each ger was reserved for women, who used the space for cooking, making clothes and looking after their children.

MONGOL CONQUESTS

Mongols conquered north China in 1215, then advanced west, reaching Russia in 1237 and Austria in 1242. They went on to conquer most of the Middle East, capturing the splendid Muslim city of Baghdad in 1258 and heading south towards the Holy Land. They were stopped by Muslim troops from Egypt, who defeated them at Ain Jalut, south of Jerusalem, in 1260. After this setback, the Mongols never properly regained their power.

Genghis Khan is proclaimed Emperor in his tent by Rashid al-Din, in a Persian literary text

GENGHIS KHAN

Genghis Khan (seated, left) ruled the largest empire the world had ever seen. It stretched right across Asia, from the Pacific Ocean to the Black Sea. He was famous for his bravery and brutality – he murdered all his half-brothers, so they would not challenge his rule! His tactics were ruthless. Anyone who stood against Mongol soldiers was killed, or enslaved if they surrendered. After Genghis Khan died, his sons and grandsons divided the Mongol Empire between themselves. It was slowly weakened by their power squabbles.

A foot soldier (left) wore
armour made of metal
splints and carried a
battle-axe and a strong
iron shield.

FRONTIER FIGHTERS

The western frontiers of Europe were protected by the sea, but European armies had to fight against enemies who threatened border lands in the north, east and south. In northern Europe, Christian soldiers, led by German Crusaders known as the Teutonic knights, clashed with pagan races living around the shores of the Baltic Sea. In the far south, Spanish troops attacked and conquered Muslim kingdoms in southern Spain, forcing all Muslims (and Jews) to leave by 1492. Along the eastern frontier, Russian princes fought against Mongol invasions and pagan tribes from Lithuania.

Around 1300, a new dynasty threatened Europe's eastern frontier – the Muslim Ottomans. Based in Turkey, they were led by the warrior Sultan Othman I (ruled 1299-1326). In 1453, his descendant Sultan Mehmed II ('the Conqueror') captured the rich Byzantine capital city of Constantinople – alarming proof of Ottoman power.

SELJUK TURKS

Seljuk sultans recruited soldiers from many different Middle Eastern lands. They all fought with their own local weapons. The horsemen (left) came from western Iran and wore armour made of chain mail and overlapping metal scales. They carried a long lance and a short sword, with a round shield slung over the shoulder. The foot soldiers came from Greece and wore a chain mail shirt, a cloth tunic and trousers.

Sword

Round shield

15th-century Turkish conical turban helmet decorated with Arabic script and chain mail

RUSSIAN CAVALRYMEN

This 14th-century Russian horseman (below) is armed to fight against Mongol invaders.

Spear and banner

Ridged shield designed to deflect blows

DEFENDING THE NORTH-EAST

In 1380, Russian Grand Prince Dmitri Ivanovich (below) won a famous victory against Tatar tribesmen. The battle began with a duel between two Tatar and Russian champions. Both were killed. Then soldiers from both sides joined in. After four hours Prince Dmitri gave orders for the Russian cavalry to charge. The Tatars fled in terror.

RIVALS

Medieval rulers won power by fighting and killing their rivals. Usually, kings came from noble families, but at the start of the Middle Ages kingship did not automatically pass from a royal father to his eldest son. When a king died, his brothers, sons, cousins and top generals might all try to seize the throne.

A soldier's banner showed which side he belonged to.

WARS OF THE ROSES
Between 1455 and 1485 rival noble families, the Yorks and the Lancasters, fought for the English throne. The conflict ended after Lancastrian Henry Tudor won the battle of Bosworth Field in 1485. He then married Elizabeth of York, uniting the two families.

Neighbouring nations could also be rivals. England and France were bitter enemies for over 100 years. Their quarrel began when the English king, Edward III (ruled 1327-1377), attacked France and claimed the throne because his mother was a French princess. At first English armies were successful, but the French slowly fought back and drove English soldiers out of most of France. They were helped by a peasant girl, Joan of Arc (1412-1431). She led French troops to victory at Orleans in 1429, but was betrayed and sold to the English, who burned her at the stake (right).

CHARLES THE WISE

King Charles V of France (ruled 1364-1380) led his armies to victory against English soldiers during the Hundred Years War (1337-1453). He took over the government of France aged only 19, after his father was captured by the English in 1356.

NATIONAL HERO

As a young man, Henry V of England (ruled 1413-1422) defeated rebels at Shrewsbury, refusing to leave the battlefield although he was badly injured. In 1415, he re-started the Hundred Years War against France and won a famous victory at Agincourt.

WICKED UNCLE

King Richard III of England (ruled 1483-1485) was supposed to protect his nephew, the young King Edward V. But Richard sent Edward and his younger brother to the Tower of London. Soon afterwards, they disappeared and Richard became king.

COMMANDER KINGS

edieval kings had to be war-leaders and fighting was their first responsibility. Victory in battle brought praise and fame, while losing a war meant death, disgrace and financial ruin. A king was judged to be 'good' if he was brave and knew how to command troops. But if a ruler was weak, cowardly, or defeated, like King John of Scotland (ruled 1292-1296), he might soon lose his throne.

Kings also needed to be able to inspire the men who fought for them with hope and courage. Most medieval armies were recruited, paid and organised by kings and their officials. A good leader, like Richard the Lionheart, could persuade his troops to follow him into the most difficult and dangerous situations.

Reverse of the royal seal of Henry II (1133-1189), depicting the armed king on horseback

WILLIAM THE CONQUEROR
William (left) became Duke of Normandy in 1035, when he was only eight years old. For the rest of his life, he was involved in wars against rival nobles and rebels in France. After conquering England in 1066, he faced revolts by English nobles. In 1073, William returned to France to try and win more land. After this he attacked Wales and fought off a Viking invasion. He died in 1087, after falling from his horse.

KING IN COUNCIL

Kings could not rule by themselves. They needed trusted advisors to help them and to govern their kingdoms while they were away fighting wars. They set up royal councils, staffed by nobles, judges, top officials and Church leaders to help plan government policy.

FREDERICK

Nicknamed 'Barbarossa' (Red Beard), Frederick (left) was King of Germany and Holy Roman Emperor from 1152 to 1190. He led a Crusader army towards the Holy Land, but drowned crossing a river before he got there.

RICHARD I

King Richard of England (left, ruled 1189-1199) was a famous warrior, nicknamed 'the Lion-Heart' for his bravery and fighting skills. He spent most of his reign away from England, fighting in the Crusades.

ROGER II

King Roger of Sicily (ruled 1105-1154) conquered lands in Italy and forced the Pope to accept him as ruler there. Then, after the Byzantine Emperor insulted his ambassador, he attacked Byzantine lands in Yugoslavia, Greece and North Africa.

19th-century painting of Roger II entering Palermo, Sicily

RUGIERRO AL PALERMO

c. 1066   c. 1160   c. 1265   c. 1300   c. 1385   c. 1450

KNIGHTS

Knights were the backbone of all medieval armies. They were well-trained, heavily-armoured soldiers who fought on horseback. Senior knights served as officers in royal armies, or as military advisors to kings. The first knights were just rough, tough fighting men, valued for their skill in battle. But after around AD 1200, knights were more highly respected. They had the right to be called 'Sir' (their wives were called 'Dame') and to wear a coat of arms (a special badge showing their family symbol).

CODES OF CONDUCT
Pictured on a painted shield (above), a young knight offers vows of loyalty and devotion to his lady-love. Knights were meant to follow the rules of chivalry and courtly love.

TOURNAMENTS
Tournaments (right) were mock battles fought with blunted weapons. Originally held as training for war, they soon became popular entertainments. Jousting was a favourite with the crowds.

Basinet helmet

Neck guard

Pauldron

Besagew

Cowter

Culet

Vambrace

Mitten gauntlets

Tasset

Greave

Sabaton

Cuirass

Cuisse

Poleyn

Knights spent many years in training, learning horseriding, battle skills and all the rules of 'courtly' (elegant and gracious) behaviour. They also acted as pages and squires (personal assistants) to the noble who was training them. Pages served food and ran errands; squires looked after a knight's horse, weapons and armour, and went with him into battle.

Beneath his armour a knight wore a doublet lined with satin and a pair of trousers called hose. Strips of material were tied around his knees to stop the armour rubbing and chain mail covered vital areas. By 1400 the development of plate armour was complete.

Polished steel armour (left) made in Milan, Italy

FIGHTING ON HORSEBACK

*H*orses were essential for medieval warfare. In battle, rows of mounted knights lined up, holding lances in the 'couched' position – pointing straight ahead and braced against their chests. As they galloped forwards their lances knocked enemy knights off their own horses, where they could be trampled to death along with nearby foot soldiers, or slashed with swords.

FOR WEALTHY WARRIORS
Only the rich could afford warhorses, which were extremely expensive. In 1337, Edward III of England paid £168 for one. At 14th-century prices, that equalled 80 years' income for a peasant family!

Lance

Shield

Caparison

Sometimes the tactic of charging failed disastrously. In 1314 English knights charging towards Scottish soldiers at the Battle of Bannockburn became trapped in a bog. Knights were also at risk as soon as they fell or dismounted from their horses. Their heavy armour weighed them down and made them easy to pick off.

STRONG AND STEADY

Knights and their horses faced a deadly shower of enemy arrows (below). Warhorses had to be strong, in order to carry the weight of a knight in his armour. They also had to be good-tempered – a nervous horse might panic and bolt. Only male horses were ridden by knights, because medieval people believed that their aggressive nature made them ideally suited for war.

Reconstruction of a horse's chanfron (head-armour), dating from 15th-century Germany

Sword

Coat of arms

Armet helmet

CASTLES

Over the centuries, castles became splendid homes for wealthy nobles and knights, but the first castles were built as forts to protect soldiers fighting in enemy territory. These forts were made of earth and timber. Most had a timber tower, surrounded by a spiked wooden fence, a steep earth bank and a deep ditch. By around 1100, castles were often built on a motte with a separate bailey nearby. After around 1150, castles were made of stone, which was much stronger than wood and did not burn. Castles all had tall keeps, or donjons. Originally these were square, but soon the design was changed and round keeps were preferred. Round keeps had no corners to get in the way of defenders shooting arrows. By 1200, castle keeps were protected by rings of thick stone walls, lookout towers and massive gateways. Many castles were surrounded by deep moats, or perched on rocky crags, to make them even more difficult to attack.

Arrow slits

Machicolations

Crenellations

Bodiam Castle (below), in southern England, was one of the last medieval castles to be built. Unlike earlier castles, where the inner fortification was protected by an encircling wall, at Bodiam chambers were built into the walls themselves. By 14th-century standards, the castle had very comfortable living quarters, and was a grand residence as well as a strong fortress.

MOTTE AND BAILEY

Early castles were of the motte and bailey style, with a wooden keep as the home of the lord or noble, built on a tall mound (the motte). This made it difficult to attack and easy to defend. Beneath the motte, the bailey was inhabited by peasants and contained essential buildings, such as stables, grain-stores and workshops for carpenters and craftsmen.

Moat

CASTLE UNDER SIEGE

astles were very difficult to attack and once castles were built of stone, they became very difficult to burn down. Knights on horseback could not harm them and it was almost impossible for soldiers to climb over their walls. If defenders saw attackers trying to breach the walls, they could easily push them off with long forked poles. Medieval armies therefore used siege warfare to try to capture castles. Castles were surrounded and cut off from the outside world so that no food, weapons, or information could enter. The same siege techniques were also used to attack walled cities and towns.

Trebuchets (right) were used to hurl huge rocks at castle walls. A similar siege engine was a ballista, which was a sort of giant crossbow.

Trebuchet

Illustration by William of Tyre showing Crusaders bombarding the besieged city of Nicaea (in present-day Turkey) with the heads of captured soldiers.

GERM WARFARE
Besiegers terrorised the people trapped inside cities and castles by shooting rotting meat or dead bodies over the walls to spread disease.

Battering rams (below) were used to bash down the castle gates. They were covered in thick animal hides to protect the soldiers moving them into position.

Battering ram

Siege towers could be constructed out of harm's way and then moved alongside city or castle walls, enabling soldiers to climb over them.

Siege tower

The longer a castle held out against a siege, the worse its inhabitants would be treated if they were captured. Attacking armies often sent heralds (official messengers) into castles to persuade defending troops to surrender, or to threaten them with a dreadful death if they refused to give in.

Ballista

Siege tower

Trebuchet

Ladder

Shield to protect archers

FOOT SOLDIERS

Most men in medieval armies were ordinary soldiers who fought on foot. They came from the poorest groups in society and sometimes volunteered for an army just to survive. In towns they formed militias to defend their homes, workplaces and families. But more often, they were forced to fight by a king's recruiting officers or their local lords.

In the early Middle Ages, foot soldiers were no match for knights on horseback. When knights charged, they fled for their lives. But after around 1300, foot soldiers became very dangerous. They used new weapons to attack knights, especially longbows, crossbows, war-flails and pikes.

14th-century longbow

14th-century crossbow

Some crossbows (above) were so big and powerful that the archer needed to use a windlass to pull back the bowstring. Crossbow bolts could pierce armour.

Longbows (above) became popular with European soldiers around 1300. The largest were as tall as a man. An arrow from a longbow could hit a target over 300 metres away.

The Battle of Crecy depicted in a 15th-century illustration from the Netherlands

Comment le roy f France fut descont

BLOODY BATTLE
Foot soldiers armed with bows and arrows fought for their lives at the Battle of Crecy in 1346 (above). In battles before the 14th century, casualties were often small, but now arrows and bolts from longbows and crossbows – the new weapons – killed thousands of men in a single day.

MEN-AT-ARMS

Foot soldiers had several ways of fighting against mounted knights. Sometimes they lured the knights into dangerous territory with hidden obstacles such as ditches and streams. Sometimes the soldiers dug pits and filled them with spikes. Sometimes, very bravely, they stood firm with pikes pointing forwards as knights charged towards them. The horses were unable to stop and were stabbed or cut to pieces as they crashed into the line of razor-sharp pikes. Archers used similar deadly tactics to fire at advancing knights.

SOLDIERS IN TRAINING
Well-trained foot soldiers were recruited by nobles to join their own special fighting units, called 'lances'. Most nobles liked to set off to war with a large team of support staff.

English archers

French knights

English and French troops fighting on a bridge, from Froissart's Chronicles, a 15th-century manuscript

FLEXIBLE FIGHTERS

In the illustration above, English soldiers (advancing from the right) attack a bridge in France during the Hundred Years War. Foot soldiers armed with daggers, swords and pikes could fight in situations where knights on horseback were useless. Defenders who stood firm in tight formation (like the French troops in the illustration) usually won battles. Once foot soldiers broke ranks, they were easier to kill individually.

LONGBOW MASSACRE

The battle of Crecy in 1346 (see painting on previous page and below) was won by English longbowmen, who slaughtered French knights and Genoese crossbowmen as they advanced. Over 1,500 French horsemen were killed. Only 40 English soldiers died. Skilled longbowmen could shoot ten arrows a minute. The arrows fell like deadly rain, causing serious injuries.

ARMY ON THE MARCH

Getting troops to the battlefield was one of the biggest challenges faced by army commanders in medieval times. Fighting men had to march on foot to where they were needed, carrying their clothes, weapons and food.

Extra equipment, such as tents, blankets, armour, arrows, spare horseshoes, wheat to make bread, cooking pots, salt meat or fish and medical supplies were carried on wooden carts or by pack-horses. In good weather, an army could travel about 19 km per day. Heavy rains, which made the ground muddy, deep snow and ice made long marches extremely difficult. In most of Europe, fighting stopped during the winter. In hostile territory, slow progress made a marching army an easy target for enemy attack.

Army commanders provided basic rations, but troops had to find much of their own food. Life on the march could be very hard. More soldiers probably died from cold, sunstroke, exhaustion and disease than on the battlefield.

As soldiers marched through villages, they would demand food and money from the peasants. If they refused, their homes might be set on fire (below), or even worse, they might be killed.

The looting of Jerusalem by Christians in 1099

GRABBING LOOT
Once they had captured a town or city, victorious armies took everything they could carry and destroyed the rest. In many cases they killed civilians, including elderly people, women and children.

The illustration from a 13th-century French manuscript (opposite) shows a medieval interpretation of the biblical story of King David. In the top half he marches with his army delivering provisions, while in the lower half he faces Goliath.

ꝟali dauit ueniens i̇ castra cum offere uellet que attulerat. audito clamore acierum que
ad pugnam parate erant dimittit omnia ad sarcinas ꝑistorum sub manu custodis ꝟ ipe
ꝓꝑaut uadit ad locum prelij ~

ꝟalter cum Dauit ueni̇ss ad locum ꝯtaminis et ille gigas more solito exꝓbraret. atꝗ oı͛s
ꝺᵗⁱ cum ualde timeret. unus dixit ꝗ quicuⁿꝗ illū post̄ occidere. rex ei filiam suam cū diuicijs
multis daret. atꝗ cum et ꝺm̄ domū patris suı imunem faceret a tributo. qd audiens Dauit.
et de conditionibᵒ ill̄ diligenter interrogans: cum omnia ꝺdiciss̄ contempsit illum gigantem ꝛ
ꝺe uictoria se habere optımam spem ostendit. k̄ fratres cū suı grauiter increpuerunt.

EASY LANDINGS
Early warships were built with shallow hulls. These could sail close inshore and land on beaches. Low gunwhales made it easy for men and horses to climb over the side and wade ashore.

FIGHTING AT SEA

There were no national navies in the Middle Ages. Only sea-trading cities such as Venice, and rich monarchs, such as the king of France, kept large fleets. Other medieval kings, including Henry V of England, 'borrowed' fighting ships from pirates, or used ships originally designed for trade to transport armies to places of war. Ferrying valuable war-horses was especially difficult. Cargo ships were often slow and cumbersome, with no suitable space for animals on board. In wartime kings often forced sea-faring communities along the coast to hand over their best ships, along with their crews.

Early medieval ships were powered by rowing, only hoisting a sail when the wind was blowing in the right direction. Later medieval ships had larger sails and could travel further at faster speeds.

CLOSE COMBAT
Once they had sailed close to an enemy ship, attackers clawed hold of it with iron grappling hooks and shot pointed arrows at its sails to rip them, or leapt on board to fight with swords.

Crusader ships sailing to the Middle East

a) 1200-1300
Vessel, developed
from Viking
warship, with
fighting platforms
at prow and stern

b) 1200-1300
North-European
warship with deeper
hull, powered by
large square sail

c) 1300-1400
Warship with deep
hull and fighting
platforms

d) 1300-1400
Mediterranean war
galley, rowed with
oars

e) 1400-1500
Three-masted,
square-rigged ship,
developed from
cargo vessels with
deep hulls

ASTROLABE
Medieval sailors used this navigation instrument (left) to work out their position at sea. It measured the height of the sun above the horizon. From this, they could calculate how far north or south they were.

Fighting platforms

Crow's nest to keep a lookout

Large sails

WARSHIP DESIGN
After around 1400, large ships with deeper hulls were built for fighting (right), especially in stormy north-European waters. They could not be rowed, so were fitted with several large sails.

14th-century knights attempt to land their warship on the coastline.
They fire a shower of arrows at the soldiers defending.

There were several medieval methods of destroying enemy ships: holing and sinking them using an underwater ram; spraying them with lime (which blinded crews); slippery soap (which made sailors fall overboard); or 'Greek Fire' (a sticky mixture that burned everything it touched). Attackers also bombarded ships with rocks, used mirrors to reflect sunlight and dazzle the steersman, and sent fire-ships (old ships, filled with tar and set alight) towards enemy craft in harbour.

FIGHTING FOR MONEY

Long pike

Hand-held gun

After around 1300, there were two important changes to the way medieval wars were fought. New kinds of soldiers were recruited and new war machines were invented. The new soldiers were mercenaries – soldiers who fought for money. Many had special skills with weapons such as crossbows. New weapons of the time were bronze and iron cannon, and smaller hand-held guns. Mercenaries organised themselves into private armies, each containing several thousand men. They chose their own leaders, who became powerful warlords, threatening to lay waste to whole districts if they did not get their own way. Mercenaries would fight for anyone who paid them, in Europe or beyond, and often changed sides. They had very different ideas about lordship and loyalty to knights in earlier times, who fought only for the king or local lord who recruited them.

Long, two-handed sword
(called a 'cat-gutter')

HIRED KILLERS

German *landsknechts* (mercenary soldiers), from around 1500 (right), were armed with typical late-medieval Swiss and German weapons. The best mercenary troops were respected for their discipline and training. Like archers, they were able to defeat a charge by knights on horseback. During the 15th century, armies, battles and numbers of casualties all became larger as rulers throughout Europe hired extra troops of mercenaries to fight alongside their own soldiers. Good mercenaries were expensive, but they often guaranteed victory.

Angel coin

From c. 1500, warships were fitted with cannon.
Their muzzles stuck out through specially-cut holes
(known as 'gun-ports') in the hull.

GUNNER'S PAY
A gold 'Angel' coin, minted
around 1520, was a month's
wages for a gunner on the
Mary Rose.

The Mary Rose,
*an English
gunship launched
in 1511*

Rigging

*Canvas
sail*

Mast

Wooden hull

Gun-port

Cannon

SMASHING!
Huge cannon (left) were also
used in sieges from around 1400.
Cannonballs could smash
through stonework, so no castle
or city could withstand their
power. On the battlefield,
smaller, marble-sized balls fired
by hand-held guns ripped into
flesh and shattered bones.

EXPLOSIVE POWER
Cannon and guns worked in the
same way. Their barrels were
packed with gunpowder and
loaded with stone or iron
balls. When the powder was set
alight, it exploded, shooting the
ball outwards with
tremendous force.

Early cannon

A GOOD WAR?

Medieval warfare was often brutal, but it was not entirely lawless. Religious leaders laid down rules for war. These declared that peace was the ideal condition for humans to live in and that wars should only be fought to defend people, places or religious ideas. Any war should be formally declared, so that enemies had the chance to start peace negotiations. Some medieval thinkers believed that if a war was fought in a good cause, then any tactics could be used. Others argued that ordinary people without weapons should be left unharmed. They also forbade looting and the deliberate destruction of enemy property. Sadly, these rules were not often obeyed.

HOLY LAWS, HOLY WARS
A messenger kneels before the Pope, head of the Catholic Church in Rome (above). Church leaders were very influential. They took sides in religious quarrels and called for wars against non-believers.

RELIGIOUS TEACHERS
Priests, monks (left) and nuns were the best-educated people in Christian Europe. They studied the Bible and other holy texts and wrote religious books of their own. Many of them spent years thinking and writing about good and bad wars.

THREE WISE MEN
Muslim scholars (above) preached 'Jihad' – a holy struggle to achieve perfection in personal behaviour and public affairs. But their words were misunderstood by some Muslim soldiers, who used them as an excuse to attack all non-Muslims.

During the Middle Ages, many thousands of soldiers and civilians died in wars. Homes and farms were destroyed, along with beautiful religious buildings and the treasures they contained. Why did this happen? Partly because kings, commanders and soldiers on all sides were greedy for wealth and power. Partly because soldiers were very hard to control, especially in the heat of battle. Most importantly of all, because leaders of medieval society believed it was their duty to fight, even if they lost their own lives.

KNIGHTS OF GOD?
Templar knights (right) spent their lives battling against Muslim armies in the Holy Land.

*Murder of Thomas Becket,
from a 13th-century book of Psalms*

UNHOLY VIOLENCE

In 1170, four knights murdered Archbishop Thomas Becket (left) in his cathedral at Canterbury, in England, after Becket quarrelled with King Henry II. This shocked many people. They honoured Becket as a saint and made pilgrimages to pray at his tomb.

REST IN PEACE

A knight's family mourns beside his tomb (above). Fighting and farm accidents were the most common cause of death for men in the Middle Ages. Many Christians (and Muslims) believed that soldiers who died fighting for their faith would be rewarded in heaven.

WARRIOR'S REWARD

An effigy of a 15th-century knight (below). Wealthy medieval men paid for images of themselves wearing armour to be placed above their tombs. They hoped to be remembered as brave warriors.

TIMESPAN

c. 900-1000

The first castles are built in France, Germany and northern Italy, as bases for soldiers. They are made of wood, surrounded by earth ramparts and ditches.

Motte and bailey castle

1066

Under the command of Duke William, Normans from France invade England and kill English King Harold at the Battle of Hastings.

Bayeux tapestry

1071

Seljuk Turks, Muslims from Central Asia led by Alp Arslan, defeat the Byzantine army at the Battle of Manzikert. They begin to rule in Turkey and seek new conquests in lands to the west.

1095

Pope Urban II calls for a Crusade to help defend Byzantine and Middle Eastern lands from Seljuk Turks. Between 1096 and 1271, there are eight major crusading expeditions.

Templar knight

1099

Crusaders capture the holy city of Jerusalem and set up kingdoms in the Middle East. These survive until Jerusalem is recaptured by Muslim troops led by Saladin in 1187.

1100-1250

Most castles are now built of stone, with massive keeps. Favourite weapons are short bows and arrows, medium length swords, used for slashing, battle-axes and spears. Armour is made from chain mail. Helmets are cone-shaped, sometimes with nose-protectors, or massive 'great helms'. A common tactic is a charge by knights on horseback. Siege warfare is also popular.

1189-1192

Campaigns of Richard the Lion-Heart (King Richard I of England) in the Holy Land.

Mongol leader

1200-1300

'The Mongol century'. In 1206, Genghis Khan becomes Mongol leader. Mongol troops set out to conquer a vast empire, stretching from China to Eastern Europe. They capture Russia in 1239, invade Hungary and Poland in 1241 and overrun Baghdad in 1258. Their advance westwards is halted by Muslim troops at the Battle of Ain Jalut, near Jerusalem, in 1260.

1212

Battle of Las Navas de Tolosa. Spanish King Peter of Aragon defeats Muslim princes in southern Spain. All Muslims and Jews are finally driven out of Spain in 1492.

1229

Teutonic knights begin campaigns against pagan peoples in Prussia and around the Baltic Sea. These end in 1387, when Lithuania becomes Christian.

1277-1283

King Edward I of England conquers Wales and builds 10 magnificent new castles there. Many are 'concentric' in design, with several sets of walls around a central donjon. In 1286, Edward I starts wars to conquer Scotland, but fails.

Beaumaris Castle

1300-1500
Longbows are now widely used and revolutionise warfare. Their arrows kill men and horses over a long range. They can be fired repeatedly and very fast. Crossbows, which are slower but very powerful, are also used on battlefields and in siege warfare. A popular battle tactic is to 'rain' arrows against advancing knights. There is an increased use of mercenaries.

Longbow archers

1300-1500
Ottoman Turks take control of former Seljuk lands and invade the Balkans, Middle East and North Africa.

1300-1500
Massive two-handed swords now used by foot soldiers. They were the largest European swords ever made.

1337-1453
The Hundred Years War between England and France. It includes many famous battles, such as Crecy (1346) and Agincourt (1415).

Plate armour

1400-1500
Armour is now made of shaped plates of metal, carefully joined together. Helmets are 'kettle-shaped', like an upturned cooking pot. New weapons include halberds (pikes), cannon and hand-held guns.

1400-1500
Castles decline in usefulness and importance, as new cannon can smash through stone walls, towers, gate-houses and donjons.

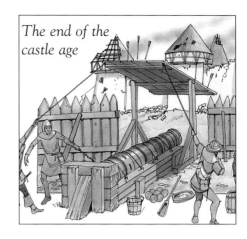

The end of the castle age

1453
Ottoman Turks capture Constantinople, the capital city of the Byzantine Empire, using guns to destroy city walls and gates.

Ottoman Turks

1455-1485
The Wars of the Roses between rival nobles in England. One of many struggles between rival dynasties throughout Europe during the late Middle Ages.

1500
New ships designed with gun-ports so they can carry cannon and fire 'broadsides' at the enemy.

GLOSSARY

Alliance A friendly agreement.

Angles People from Germany and Denmark who settled in Britain from around AD 400.

Armet helmet A light helmet with a neck guard and visor.

Ballista A giant crossbow.

Byzantine An empire in Greece and Turkey, powerful from around AD 600-1453.

Celts People who lived in the north and west of Europe in Roman times and previously.

Chivalry The medieval custom of polite, honourable behaviour.

Coat of arms A design – with special colours, patterns or symbols – worn by members of a noble family and their soldiers.

Concentric A castle with more than one set of surrounding walls.

Courtly Elegant and gracious.

Crenellation A rampart built around the top of a castle with regular gaps for firing arrows.

Crossbow A powerful weapon that fired short, thick arrows or metal bolts.

Crusades Wars fought between Christians and Muslims.

Effigy A lifelike statue of a dead person.

Estate A large area of land owned by one family.

Fealty Loyalty and obedience.

Franks People who lived in northern France from around AD 500.

Ger A Mongol family's felt tent.

Jihad An Arabic word meaning 'struggle'.

Knights Expert, well-trained warriors, usually from noble families.

Machicolation Openings in a castle wall through which stones and boiling liquids can be dropped on attackers.

Mameluk Well-trained Muslim soldiers, based in Egypt, originally recruited from slaves.

Mercenaries Soldiers who would fight for anyone who paid them.

Militia A local army.

Moat A deep ditch filled with water.

Mongols Nomad peoples who lived in Central Asia.

Mosque A building used by Muslims for prayer.

Nomads People who regularly move their homes.

Ottoman Turks Muslim people who ruled an empire based in Turkey from around 1300.

Pagan Word used by Muslims and Christians to describe non-believers.

Pilgrims People who make journeys to visit holy places.

Saxons People who lived in southern Germany in the 5th and 6th centuries.

Scutage Tax paid to avoid becoming a knight.

Sermon A religious speech.

Slavs People who lived in Russia and eastern Europe.

Squire A young man, training to be a knight, who worked as a knight's personal assistant.

Steppes Dry, windswept grassland.

Surcoat The long cloth robe worn on top of armour.

Templar knights Crusader knights whose task it was to guard the captured city of Jerusalem.

Trebuchet A machine that hurled rocks.

War-flail Spiked balls on chains, which were used to hit the enemy.

Windlass A winding machine.

INDEX

Page numbers in **bold** refer to illustrations.